Ultimate Power
Enemy
Within the Ranks

Linda A. Fischer

Unlimited Inc.
Honolulu

Disclaimer

The events described in this story are true. There are no fictional or composite characters, although the identity of some figures and their descriptions have been changed,due to right to privacy concerns. Any similarity drawn between these fictitious names and those of actual persons is coincidental.

Published by:
Unlimited Incorporated
P.O. Box 89546
Honolulu, Hawaii 96830-9546
tel: 808.921.9005
website: www.unlimited-inc.com

International Standard Book Number: 0-9666350-0-0
Library of Congress Catalog Card Number: 98-96494

Cover illustration by Anna Barrera
Book design by Joan Ryan

10   9   8   7   6   5   4   3   2   1

265/2/90

Dedicated to the victims of sexual assault,
past, present and future.
May you find peace and enjoy the happiness
life has to offer.

I share these words with you as you search
for closure.

God is our refuge and strength,
a very present help in trouble.

Psalm 46:1

Kim,

Thanks for all your support. I could not have done it without you.

Acknowledgments

I would like to acknowledge the enormous help given me in completing this book.

To Nancy Lundsgaard, a superb editor, and Joan Ryan, graphic designer extraordinarie: I thank you both for your encouragement, enthusiasm, and support which made this book a reality; to the friends, you know who you are, whose support was a great source of strength: I thank you all; to those so very close to me, my family, with whom I laugh and dream and find peace and love: a heartfelt thanks for your love and support; and to Jim, the treasure in my life, with your unfailing wisdom, patience, and love: thank you for the countless riches you bring to me.

Foreword

If a woman wanted to serve in the military before the 20th Century, it was necessary to pass her off as a man. Even when faced with massive manpower shortages during WWII the concept of using women to release men for combat proved to be a real battle. Army leaders and Congress didn't want women in the "real" military so at first they let them enlist in a Women's Army Auxiliary Corps. The women did an incredible job and it became desirous and necessary to get them into the established Army. Then a "slander campaign" began. It started with simple patronizing humor. Then a serious news report was written that WAACs were issued prophylactics in order to perform the duties for which they were really recruited. Finally they were nicknamed "Prostitutes in Khaki."

This seriously affected enlistment and almost derailed the whole program. However, women did succeed in making a place for themselves in the military. In 1943, the Women's Army Corps was established, and in 1978 the WACs were disestablished as a separate group and women were officially integrated into the regular Army. It's been a tough predicament for women from the start.

Major Linda Fischer is a young woman in today's Army. She has written an incredible, personal account of her ordeal within that organization. It reads like a good mystery novel but it's all true. She was a victim of sexual harassment by one man, then a victim of a dismissive and insensitive bureaucracy. It's obvious that the seeds of what she encountered were planted during WWII. There has never been enough training given to either men or women to cope with each other in a military setting.

In 1924, right after WWI, a report written by Major Everett Hughes predicted many of the problems that would be experienced by the Army. He had been assigned to study the possibility of using women in future conflicts. He advised that women would be integral to the Army and that they should be embraced within the current system. That men and women should be given considerable training, otherwise you'd have "men not knowing how to lead women, and women not knowing how to be led by men."

The recurring sex scandals in the military indicate that there are still lessons to learn from Major Hughes' report, and now another major adds her words of wisdom. She points out the potential danger of the military's current system and policies, which are inadequate to handle situations in the new Army. In her case, a commanding officer did not think of her as a fellow soldier. Outdated thinking like that and the old order that supports such behavior must fall to the side, and Major Fischer has concrete ideas to make things better.

Vera S. Williams
WACs: Women's Army Corps 1942 to 1978
WASPs: Women Airforce Service Pilots of WWII

Word of Introduction

During a visit to Texas to visit my family, I sat in the warmth of the sun, physically and mentally exhausted from my experiences as a victim of sexual assault in the military. My father came out to sit with me, and we talked quietly of what lay ahead for me. Although uncertain of my own future, I knew I had to find a way to help other women in the military.

"I don't want anyone else to go through what I have," I said, "so I'm thinking about writing a book."

That conversation was two years ago and writing this book has been a long, difficult process. Turning my memories into words on paper has meant reliving painful memories. Even today, when I think back to the Panama night that changed my life, I feel a cold chill. But my determination to make a difference hasn't waivered.

Unfortunately, this story doesn't have a completely happy ending. The military system never did afford me the justice I believe I deserved. And while recent sex scandals have forced the military to take a closer look at the problem of sexual assault and harassment, changing deeply ingrained attitudes and practices will take a long-term commitment from those at the very top. I hope this book will be seen as one more voice advocating for those changes. However, whether the system changes or not, I'll consider the book a success if it keeps just one woman from becoming a victim, or helps equip one woman with the tools to resist harassment.

Finally, the process of writing what you are about to read has brought healing and growth for me personally. I feel a sense of closure; my story has been told.

Contents

Ultimate Power

Enemy
Within the Ranks

Linda A. Fischer

A journey begins. . .

Specialist Linda A.Fischer   1982

Major Linda A. Fischer   1997

And today. . .

Linda and Jim in Honolulu   *1998*

Why Can't I Say No?

The night air was unusually hot and humid, even for Panama City—steamy as a sauna. Inside the Non-Commissioned Officers' Club, where I stood drinking my fourth beer, the temperature was a cool sixty-five degrees, but I felt as if the heat from outside had followed me in. I knew my light brown complexion was glowing with a hot redness, flushed from the alcohol I had consumed in the last hour. And under my battle fatigues, dampness soaked my body. Thank God my long brown hair was pinned up—the thick, wavy strands off my neck.

It was another Friday "hail and farewell" social, an opportunity for Lieutenant Colonel Harold Smith, my immediate superior, to bid goodbye to soldiers returning to the States and to welcome newcomers. He expected me to attend, like all the officers in his command. But, unlike the others, he expected me to stay close by his side whether I liked it or not, rather than mingle with the crowd. All evening I'd felt his pale blue eyes on me—just as they always seemed to be these days.

The beers I'd drunk this evening had done little to dowse the angry fire within me—a fire kindled by the knowledge that my commander demanded and then monopolized every free moment I had. And I had no say about it.

When Lt. Col. Smith arrived in Panama in 1992, one year into my tour there, he and I began our relationship on respectful, friendly terms. Now, eighteen months later, he treated me differently than he treated the other officers. He seemed to always want me nearby. Every day he would ask me to go running or play racquetball or come to his office for a chat even if he knew I had other obligations. He'd tell me to attend this affair or that event, and when I tried to beg off, saying I was swamped with paperwork or needed to take care of urgent details involving the unit I commanded, he would fire back some remark to remind me that *he* was the boss and that my fate in the Army rested with him.

"Yes, sir!" I'd learned to snap back in proper Army form. "What time, sir?"

Standing beside me in the dimness of the NCO Club, the slightly-built colonel seemed to tower over me. Not because of my five feet two inches or 120 pounds, but because in the shadow of his ultimate power and authority and the way he wielded it, I felt small and helpless. For some time now my normal confidence had been shriveling, my zest for life disappearing. This was a new and devastating experience for me.

For all of my thirty-two years, I'd seen myself strong like my beautiful Mexican mother and self-assured like my proud Texan father, a career military man. Growing up in a military family that moved constantly, I learned to take on bullies, even if they were bigger than me. Wherever we lived, I protected younger children, especially my little brothers, and never let anybody push them around.

Beginning in junior high, I'd grown intensely competitive, collecting awards and medals as an accomplished athlete. I was determined to succeed at everything I attempted and saw myself as an achiever, someone who could make it in life no matter what the obstacles. In fact, a teacher of mine had once admitted admiring me for never giving up on what I wanted.

What I wanted, I discovered after putting myself through college in three years, was a successful military career. And, at this time I had achieved much of the success I had hoped for. I was Captain Linda Fischer, an eleven year career officer, commander of a 220-soldier military police unit. On top of all that, I was diligently working on a master's degree in educational psychology and had won numerous Army sporting championships.

Yes, the Army seemed the perfect place for me. Because of my background, I understood and could accept aspects of Army life that bothered some people—the chain of command, the code of absolute obedience to your commander. I thrived on the competitive life style, the challenge "to be all that I could be."

Yet here I stood, feeling like my commander's

possession, like a little girl trying not to make her daddy mad. It was not a good feeling, and the beer helped keep it at bay. For months now, I'd tried not to inflame the situation, to keep my respectful distance while remaining professional and friendly. But Lt. Col. Smith persisted in focusing his attention on me at command social and sporting events. Although he knew my romantic feelings were reserved for Jim, back home in the States.

Recently, his demands had intensified, and I found myself feeling more and more powerless, unable to say *no* to him. When I did, he would fix me with a disapproving look as if he were dealing with a willful child and remind me that he held my future in his hands.

For the past few months, I'd felt increasingly on edge. Like I did tonight. I must have been on my fifth beer, although I'd never been much of a drinker before. In fact, while others downed alcoholic drinks, I could usually be found with a soft drink in my hands. But I'd learned recently that beer and rum and cokes had a dulling effect, and they had become my primary comfort during social times with the commander. Only for some reason, I wasn't the one buying tonight, as I usually did. No, someone was stacking drinks in front of me faster than I could gulp them down.

Feeling like a dog on a leash, I swiped at the dampness trickling down the back of my neck. Did the other officers talk about what was—or wasn't—going on between the commander and me, I wondered? I knew my former first sergeant, Master Sergeant Martinez, sensed my frustration and anger for he made sure to check in with me often at these gatherings. And what about Sandy, Lt. Col. Smith's wife? I suspected that she hadn't picked up on her husband's strange behavior because he seemed more cautious in her presence. She often attended "hail and farewell" socials, but where was she tonight?

I sipped a beer, my mind whirling with endless threats I could only imagine hurling at the man I'd come to see as my tormentor. My thoughts jumped from strategizing an excuse for leaving to buzzing with a light alcohol-induced dizziness. All I wanted to do was escape from the party.

Why can't I just say, "Sir, I'll be going now"? Why can't I just say it? I asked myself those questions as I sipped at yet another beer that had been plopped down in front of me. And I had no answers. All I had was the anger that I felt welling in me like a volcano—the anger that arose from feeling trapped between my attempts to placate my boss and protect my career and this strange paralysis. With no way to release my anger, at least around him and my troops, all I could do was run the anger out of me every night, with a fast paced 5 mile run before going home.

But I couldn't run now. I had to stay at his side while old, familiar arguments raged inside me. *I can't take this anymore. Yes, you can, Linda. Just go along with him. You've got 11 years under your belt now. Why jeopardize your whole career at this point? After all, you've only got six more months until you can leave Panama and the commander far behind. Your next tour of duty is bound to be better, and then you'll have just nine years until you can retire from the Army with a retirement pension and a whole 'nother life to live. Don't throw it all away now. You've achieved great success so far, and besides, you've set your sights on making major. So just stay cool!*

"Right, Captain?" Lt. Col. Smith's voice captured my attention.

"Wha..what, sir?"

"Captain, you'd better slow down. I'd hate to see you hangin' over the side of the boat tomorrow chuckin' all day instead of snaggin' a big one."

Laughter from the other officers rocked me sober enough to clear some of the buzz from my head. *The fishing trip tomorrow. I had forgotten.*

"The commander's right, ma'am." Master Sgt. Martinez whispered, gently nudging my arm. "With all due respect, ma'am, you've been acting like a zombie, and that's your, what...fifth or sixth beer? You better get yourself home."

"I'm just waiting for the right moment, know what I mean?" I gave a subtle nod towards the colonel. "Say soldier, it's almost 9:00. Shouldn't you be going? Aren't your kids waiting up for you? *You* should get going."

"Not a problem, ma'am." The worried look on Martinez' face was all too familiar these days. "But, ma'am, promise me you'll get going soon."

"Promise," I chimed.

Still doubtful, the tall, muscular sergeant turned to leave, but halted. "You sure I shouldn't wait and drive you?"

"I'll be okay, so outta here!" I whispered. "You're a good man, sergeant. You and the family have a good weekend, you hear?"

By the time the party started breaking up, I was cradling a fresh beer in my hands, not drinking much anymore but needing to hold on to something while I waited for the commander to finish his goodbyes. He'd dismissed his driver earlier and asked me to take him home. *There goes my run,* I'd thought to myself as I parroted the obligatory, "No problem, sir." *Why can't I just say no?* It wasn't unusual for one of his officers to give him a ride, but I did wish he'd asked one of the others. I desperately wanted this night to be over.

Continuing to nurse my beer, I hoped the buzz in my head would subside before I got behind the wheel of my little white Chevy. I tried to reassure myself. *At least he lives on base, not far from here. With so little traffic at this time of night, I can get him home in a few minutes and be back at my place in no time at all.* I wasn't thinking about playing it safe. All I wanted was to get the colonel home *fast* and out of my sight. Tomorrow's fishing trip would come much too soon for me.

My Nightmare Begins

In the steamy night air, I concentrated on keeping
the car on the road while the colonel chattered on about
tomorrow's fishing trip. Usually I loved fishing with my
buddies, mostly other soldiers. The Panama Canal waters
were beautiful, calm and sparkling clear, and we never came
home without our coolers emptied of food and drinks and
full of good-eating fish. But lately I'd been annoyed that the
colonel commanded me to come along rather than invite me
as I suspected he did his other subordinates.

The houses along Colonels' Row were built above
ground with the living quarters over open garages, so when I
pulled into Lt. Col. Smith's driveway, I could see his car and
the fishing boat we'd be in tomorrow, but his wife's car was
missing. *Where could Sandy be this late?*

"Come on in," the commander said. "I've got some
paperwork you need to pick up over the weekend."

I groaned inwardly. "Can't it wait, sir?" I said. "I
think I better get myself home before I get sick in your
driveway."

The colonel climbed out of his seat, ignoring my
request. "Park across the street, Captain!" he whipped. I
blinked in disbelief. It wasn't at all unusual for him to ask
his company commanders to pick up reports at his house,
but not at midnight.

I must have taken too long to respond because he
turned back toward me and said firmly, "Captain Fischer? I
think you better come get these papers."

"Yes, sir," I barked with as much respect as I could
muster. Well, if he didn't want me to park in his driveway,
at least that meant Sandy would be home soon. I backed my
car out and parked across the street. Then I headed un-
steadily for the steps that led from the garage level up to the
kitchen. *Too many beers tonight, Linda.* The alcohol really
kicked in when I began to climb the stairs, and I was forced

7

to grip the railing with both hands in order to reach the small porch outside the kitchen door.

The colonel stood in the kitchen doorway, watching me. *I'll just grab the papers and run*, I thought. *That is, if he'll let me.*

He handed me the papers, and with just one glance, I could tell this was another one of his ruses to waste my time.

"Come on in," he commanded. *Oh, no, he's not going to let me off easy tonight. Wonder what the story will be this time? Sure hope Sandy shows up soon.*

When I stepped into the small kitchen, he closed the door behind me. Then, reaching into the refrigerator, he retrieved a chilled bottle of Ballatore, my favorite champagne.

"What do you say we toast that race you pulled off this week?" he said.

The bright kitchen light increased my dizziness, and for a moment I couldn't figure out what the commander was talking about.

"I know you were hurting," he said, ripping off the bottle's wrapper, popping the cork, and then handing me one of the two champagne glasses already sitting on the counter.

Oh, yes, the race I'd run this week with a hip injury that hadn't completely healed. I braced my wobbly self against the counter and watched the colonel pour champagne into first his glass, then mine.

"So let's drink one to you for finishing!" He lifted his glass at me and took a gulp.

If I had been thinking straight, I would have said, *Sir, wouldn't the right time and place for this have been earlier this evening at the club?* After all, it wasn't unusual for a commander to toast one of his officers for outstanding accomplishments. Awards and toasts have always been important rituals in the Army—rituals designed to make you feel good for giving your life to an institution that could command you at will, any time, and under any circumstance. Races like mine last weekend weren't run for the individual but to give the organization a victory the leader could brag about. But a toast at midnight in that leader's home?

My befuddled mind did register that the last thing

I needed was another drink, but impaled by the commander's watchful eyes, I lifted my glass and took a cautious sip.

The colonel picked up the bottle from the counter. "We better talk. Things between us are getting too strained. Like tonight. You just stood there."

I wanted to fire back, *What did you want me to do? If you'd leave me alone, we'd be fine!* But I didn't. We'd had that conversation several times before. He'd say, *Captain, your conduct has been disrespectful. You're not showing me the professional courtesy that you should, and it's causing the other officers to wonder. I'm really concerned.* And I'd say, *I'm sorry, sir, I'll do better, sir,* trying not to aggravate him or start anything. But then we'd go in circles. Always the same conversation, always the same circle. Tonight I had no strength for it, so I followed him into the living room, hoping his wife would be home soon.

I perched on the living room couch as far from the commander as I could, trying to avoid his gaze. With every sip of champagne, my dizziness increased until the room spun around me. I yearned to give in to the champagne-beer mix and sink into sleep, and I fought to keep my eyes open. While I struggled to stay conscious, the colonel poured another drink for himself.

"You've changed, you know," he said, breaking the silence. "We used to get along great, and now you hardly have...some curt answer to get me off your...talk about this, Linda... not good in front of the others. They've been wondering.......they have, and I......." His voice faded in and out.

My mind drifted, my head drooped as I fought the darkness that was closing in. The room disappeared, then reappeared, then spun crazily around. I sensed he was moving closer, when blackness enveloped me.

Hands, grabbing and groping, awakened me out of my stupor. The commander was on top of me, pulling at my shirt. His lips pressed against mine. Hard. Smothering. I turned my head away and struggled to push him aside. But not powerfully enough. My shock, the confusion, the

suddenness of his attack, the alcohol, his strength—these
were his allies.

My protests weakened as I felt my mind slip again
into blackness. I don't know how long I went under, but I
awoke to find myself naked, the colonel pulling me down a
hall. I felt weak and dazed, and the walls still spun around
me. Where were my clothes? How did he get them off? I
was flat on my back on what felt like a bed. His naked body
held me down, his arms pinned mine.

"I've been waiting a long time to do this," he said,
as he planted more kisses. I fought his lips and arms, but my
struggles only made him laugh and hold me tighter. A sick
grin decorated his face when he pushed his penis against me.
I managed to reach down and shove it away, and that's when
I felt the condom he had somehow slipped on come off. I
rolled away. And the world went black again.

When I emerged from the darkness, I didn't know
where I was at first. Then the shock and horror of what had
just happened hit me. I turned to see the commander lying
on his back, his face toward me, his eyes searching mine. He
reached to pull me closer. *Oh, God.* I wanted to bolt from
the bed and run, but my shocked muscles would barely
move. All I could do was pull weakly away, wrap the sheet
around me, and slip off the bed. He didn't stop me when I
left the room.

I staggered down the hall as if I was moving through
heavy molasses, searching for the bathroom. I felt violated
and dirty, desperate to wash the nightmare away. Once
inside the bathroom, I locked the door behind me, but left
the light off, believing that only darkness could shelter me
from my shame, from my hurt. I stepped into the bathtub
and washed. The warm water pouring over me soothed me,
like my mother bathing me. *Oh Mama, oh Mama*, I cried
inside as my soapy hands touched and washed the hurt. My
head pounded and my body ached. Yet a part of me felt
strangely numb. *This didn't happen. This did not happen!* I
repeated to myself.

When the full consciousness of where I was and
who else was in the house hit me, I panicked. Quickly I

turned the water off and stepped out of the tub, fumbling for a towel, any towel, to wrap around my nakedness. I had to escape from this house. Then I heard the wooden floor outside the bathroom creak with footsteps. I clutched the towel tightly around me, every part of my body tensing with fear.

"There are clothes outside the door for you," I heard the commander say.

Like a small, trapped animal, I didn't move, but listened for what he would do next. Finally footsteps moved away from the bathroom, and after waiting for a few minutes, I opened the door and reached for the pile of clothes. I could see they were his clothes—a pair of shorts and a T-shirt, and if I'd been myself, I might have refused to put them on. But I didn't care whose clothes I wore, if only I could get away. I slipped into the clothes hurriedly, repeating to myself, *This isn't happening. This did not happen.*

When I was dressed, I opened the door cautiously, making sure the colonel wasn't lurking in the hallway before I crept out. The lights in the living room were still on, and I blinked at the wall clock that read almost 5:30 a.m. *Morning? Where is Sandy? Where did the night go?* I gathered up my clothes and boots and headed for the kitchen door. The commander was still nowhere in sight. *Thank God, thank God!* I pushed the screen door open and grabbed the handrail.

My careful steps down those stairs seemed to take forever. All the while my mind raced, trying to convince my body that the night had just been a bad dream. When I reached the bottom step, I felt a small measure of safety at last. Until I heard the commander's voice.

"Linda? Can you get the poles? Everything else is loaded." He stood in the dark driveway beside his fishing boat, blocking the way to my car.

I stared at him in disbelief. *Oh God! So that's why he put the shorts and shirt outside the door. He's expecting me to go on the fishing trip with him! I can't believe it!*

I wanted desperately to run away, but paralysis weakened my muscles. I felt like I was moving mechanically, unable to control events around me. If you've ever had a nightmare—the kind where you *know* you're dreaming but you can't wake yourself up—you know what I'm talking about. Here was this man who had just assaulted me telling me to get *fishing poles*. And I was getting them. With shock dimming my mind, I saw no way out. The only thing I knew was that "no" was not the right answer with him. But surely he would let me put my belongings in my car? I started around him.

"Linda," he barked, "I said, get the poles! Just put your stuff in the van."

I felt my lips form words but no sound emerged. The colonel opened the van door, indicating that I should shove my clothes behind the passenger seat. Then, as he had commanded, I brought him the fishing poles leaning up against one carport wall. In silence, we hooked the boat up and soon the van was pulling out of the driveway, heading off post. I closed my eyes and rested my head on the window's glass, trying to shut out the madness of this moment.

In the van, I drifted mercifully off to sleep, not waking until forty-five minutes later when the colonel was backing the van up to the Gamboa boat launch. I'd slept so deeply that when I awoke, at first I didn't remember anything was wrong. But then memories of the night flooded back, hitting me like a blow to the head. I struggled to push them away.

I must have been dreaming. Yes, it was all a bad dream.

A couple of men hanging out at the pier helped the colonel put the boat in the water. In Panama, local guys like these do everything for you—for a small price. They put the motor on the back of the boat, start it, and take the boat over to the pier where they help load. I watched them, but I felt like I was in a dream with all the action going on around me in the distance.

When the fifteen foot boat was in the water, I stepped in and sat at the front, holding the boat close to the pier while the motor idled. Automatically I checked my watch; 6:15 a.m. The colonel was driving the van to the

parking lot. When he returned, our two fishing partners—
non-commissioned officers I'd often fished with—would be
with him. And I wouldn't have to be alone with my assailant
any longer.

Oh, God, no such luck. The commander came back
alone. And before I could ask him what was going on, he
jumped into the boat, put the motor in high gear, and steered
the boat away from the dock.

"The others aren't coming," he said over the whine
of the engine.

The Survivor In Me Kicks In

The others weren't coming? I could not believe it.
They were at the club last night, and they hadn't said
anything to me. *Oh, God, the commander must have told
them that he'd canceled the trip. And he must have known
before we left the house this morning that we would be alone
all day. What's going on?*

The commander steered the boat away from the
launch area out to Lake Gautun, the forty mile lake through
which the Panama Canal and its many locks run. The
morning air cooled my face, and the lake's surface was
calm, except for the wake of the boat. Soon the sun would
rise above the rain forest to splash its glorious light on the
water and awaken the life below the surface. Watching the
sun rise usually brought me great joy. But not today.

While we passed the buoys that line the Canal and
mark the way for the hundreds of ships and boats passing
through daily, I kept my eyes down, staring into the crystal-
line water. We were heading toward Buoy 42, about forty-
five minutes away, the spot where we normally started our
fishing excursions. Often we would take up to five hours to
fish our way back. Not today, I prayed. We passed four or
five fishing boats, but I didn't boom my usual, "What's
happening? Have a great catch! See you back at the pier."
Instead, I sat stiffly in the front of the boat, my back to the
commander, wishing I could forget I was out on the water
alone. With *him.*

We motored out beyond the Barre of Colorado, an
island in the lake not far from the small cove where we
normally fished first. I loved fishing at the cove. All you had
to do was wait for the fish to start hitting. Most of the time
they struck in the same area, close to a healthy weed bed
loaded with minnows. As soon as the sun crested the top of
the rain forest, light would flash on the minnows and on the
entire cove. Then the bass would start hitting—so many that
the water would appear to be boiling. Yes, it was an incred-

ible fishing spot. But today I couldn't have cared less about
fishing. I just wanted the trip to be over.

When we arrived at our regular spot, the commander
dropped anchor. Immediately I grabbed a pole and began
fishing my end of the boat, while he fished the other end. We
didn't say a word, and the silence thickened. Soon I reeled in
my first bass, completely without my usual enthusiasm and
excitement. Everyone knew me to be a nut out on the water.
I'd laugh and talk to the fish, saying *Here, fishy, fishy,* or
I got you, baby! Now I focused all my energy on trying not
to panic. As the shock symptoms ebbed, I began to think
more rationally and to comprehend the monstrousness of the
night before. An officer forcing himself on his direct subordinate. *What should I do? Dare I report this? Would anyone
even believe me? How would this affect my career?*

After about an hour of silent fishing, I laid my pole
down, the line still trailing in the water, and reached into the
ice chest for a sandwich and a soda. I chewed slowly,
watching my line and keeping my back to the commander.
When I heard him move toward the ice chest, I felt sick with
fear that he might sit down next to me. But when I turned
my head, I saw he'd returned to the rear of the boat.

He caught my glance. "I think we should talk about
last night, Linda."

I didn't say a word. I had nothing to say.

"There are some things I want to tell you," he
continued.

At that moment a fish hit my line. I set my soda
down, straddling my seat to pull in the bass, a light green
beauty with black stripes near the tail, then mechanically
unhooked the fish and tossed it into the cooler. Out of the
corner of my eye I could see the commander waiting for me
to finish the task. How I wished I were wearing sunglasses
to hide my face from him.

His next words stunned me. "Linda, I did plan for
us to be alone today on the fishing trip." The tender look on
his face made me feel ill. "But what happened last night was
not planned. The guys called me days ago and canceled."

Canceled? The other guys canceled? If looks could

kill, the glare I turned on the commander would have silenced him forever.

Unfortunately, he kept talking. "I didn't tell you because I decided it would be a good time for us to get together and talk. I just have to tell you that over this past year, I've fallen in love with you, Linda. I've never met anyone who has so many of the same interests as me and is so accomplished at the things I am. To tell you the truth, I'm not sure I made the right decision when I married so young," he said, shaking his head, his eyes downcast now. "We were so young. Maybe we should have waited. I don't know."

The commander's words faded to a mutter. I couldn't listen anymore. Not when the silent conversation in my head was so loud. *Oh, man, this is just incredible. I can't believe he is saying this. He's my superior! He is out of control. Why don't those fish start biting again, so he'd quit talking.*

"Linda?"

I didn't respond, and the silence between us sliced the air.

"Can't you say something?" he begged. "I've got to know how you feel. I've had these feelings for some time, and I just have to know if you share them. So please tell me how you feel."

I wanted to yell at him: *Why? Why are you telling me all this?* But I knew I must use words that would put a stop to the conversation.

"Colonel, you have no right to ask. And you have no right to be telling me these things." Although I had turned my head in his direction, my eyes looked through, not at him. "My grandmother once told me that it's sometimes better not to share your feelings, that some things are better left unsaid and unknown. And I think this is one of those times." I dropped my gaze to the water.

"I guess that means you don't care for me," he said.

Oh, God, I felt trapped, what could I say? *No* was never the right answer with him. But neither was *yes.* Isolated in this secluded cove with no one around but him, I had to play it safe. If I told the truth and said, "No, I don't have feelings for you," he might tear into a rage and explode at me for not sharing his feelings. And if I said, "Yes, I do," I'd be lying just to get him off my back, and I might find him coming at me.

"Sir, I did not say that. *You* said that. What *I* said is that you have no right to ask and no need to know." The conversation felt like one more invasion, one more chance to strip me.

"Linda, please, tell me..."

"Sir, you have no right to ask!" I blurted. "Understand, it will never happen again!"

With that, he gave up his attempt to talk to me and turned to the motor, yanking the starter fiercely. We headed back to the boat launch. Normally I would have been waving to other boaters and bragging about my great catches, but now I sat in silence, my mind swirling with questions. *How could this have happened? I had none of these feelings for him. So where was this coming from? What did I do? What could have made this happen? Nightmares like this happened to other people, not to me. I was always so careful, so guarded. I'd never misled anyone. I'd never wanted or needed to.*

I thought everyone knew that I was committed to Jim, my boyfriend of several years, back in the States. When someone asked me out, I would say, *No thanks*, and that would be enough. No questions asked. Occasionally some guy would approach Millie, my best friend in Panama, and ask her about me. She would say, "Don't even waste your time. Linda has her man back in the States. She won't even give you a second look." So how did the commander get the idea that anything was possible between us when he knew I was looking forward to seeing Jim again soon?

Then it occurred to me: he didn't think he'd done anything wrong. *How could he think such a thing? A superior with his subordinate? Oh God, he's got to be out of his mind. What made him think he had the right? What if he tries something again?*

Slumped in the front of the boat, I felt helpless and trapped. How could the man who was sitting no more than five feet from me have crossed the line that is drawn so clearly for every officer in the United States Army?

At 9:30 a.m., after the shortest and most miserable fishing trip of my life, the boat slowed to a stop at the launch. Neither the colonel nor I had spoken the entire way back, and I could tell that the Panamanians who had helped load the boat were surprised to see us back so early with such a small catch.

While the commander went to get the van and trailer, I carried the fish over to the edge of the pier and counted them. It didn't take long for one of the local men to clean and fillet the few fish we had caught. Soon the commander returned, and with help from the men around us, hooked up the boat and replaced our gear in the van. Then he came over to pay the man for the cleaned fish—ten cents for each. I walked away without saying a word and climbed into the van. He was silent, too, busying himself with loading the fish into the cooler and the cooler into the van. Finally, he started the engine. When we pulled away from the launch area, I closed my eyes once more and rested my head against the window, drifting into sleep again.

Back at the colonel's house, we maintained our uneasy silence. He unloaded the fish. I reached behind the van's passenger seat to retrieve my clothes. Then I bolted for my car and pulled away without looking back. Did he watch me leave? I don't know.

On the road, I marshaled my concentration to stay focused on the road. Not that I was having a problem staying awake. But the endless chatter echoing in my head seemed to suck energy from me. *How did I, a strong, confident woman, a highly educated captain with all these people reporting to me, a champion athlete, get myself into this? How had I allowed myself to be reduced to feeling small and helpless? To be caged by such a paralyzing fear? To be caught in his game of power and control? To be intimidated by his sheer authority and position? How could I have been outsmarted and overpowered?* I had no answers.

Safe at last in my second floor apartment a few miles away from the post, I headed directly for the shower, pulling off the colonel's shorts and shirt as I went. The clothes felt contaminated, infected, and I was glad to get them off my body. Then for what seemed like hours, I stood in the shower, finally letting the tears stream down my face. No more thoughts or questions barraging me. Only waves of overpowering feelings washed over me. Fear. Shame. Hopelessness. Rage.

After my shower, I pulled a green satin house coat tightly around me. My eyes were swollen and sore, my contact lenses were glued to my corneas, and my hands shook as I removed the tiny pieces of plastic. Then I made my way into the darkened living room to open the curtains and the sliding door to a marble-tiled balcony. The blazing sun had heated my apartment to a sweltering temperature, but now a light breeze entered, bringing its welcome coolness. I turned on the TV and set the volume low.

I collapsed on the living room sofa and allowed questions to flood my mind again. *Where had Sandy been last night? Why didn't she come home? Had she been out of town? If so, where was her car? Why was my favorite champagne in the commander's refrigerator? If he hadn't planned what happened, why did he have protection on hand? And what about the beers at the club? Why had they kept coming? And from where? From him? Had he sent his driver home on purpose?* Now that I had time to think about the previous night, a lot of details weren't adding up for me.

I tortured myself with these questions until finally my survivor's instincts kicked in. I would do whatever I needed to do, even to denying the events of the previous night, to survive. *I can maneuver my way through this. I can pretend it didn't happen. I don't have to tell anyone. I'll just put walls up, protect myself, and watch my back when it comes to the commander. I can outsmart him if I have to and get myself out of this trap without sacrificing my career and all my years invested so far. I can play the game.*

Funny, during all my years in the Army, I had believed that the rules and protocols would prevent nightmares like this from happening. Not so funny, actually. For now I knew I was wrong. The rules hadn't protected me.

When I'd let my guard down, the commander had manipulated me, and I'd become his prey.

In an attempt to comfort myself, I repeated: *I can survive. I will survive.* However, what I didn't realize then—the morning after a horrific night—was that I had absolutely no idea what or who I was taking on. And I wouldn't fully realize the enormity of my situation until several years later when it turned out to be the biggest challenge of my life. A challenge I believe no soldier should have to face in the United States Army.

Curled up on my blue and white striped sofa, a breeze playing over me, I closed my eyes and cursed the day Lieutenant Colonel Harold Smith arrived in Panama.

Before the Nightmare

July, 1992. The powerful tropical sun beat down on the green parade field where First Sergeant Martinez and I waited to lead our unit onto the field. Keeping our voices low, we shared our concern that the morning heat might topple some soldiers during the upcoming Change of Command ceremony. In a few minutes, the Military Police Battalion would bid farewell to Lt. Col. Larson, a tough leader who had earned my deepest respect and taught me much. And we would welcome Lt. Col. Harold Smith, our new commanding officer and an unknown entity to most of us. Although I had only recently taken command of a military police company, I was already proud of the unit's accomplishments, and I hoped my new boss would share my feelings.

At a signal from Major Morris, the officer in charge, 1st Sgt. Martinez and I took our places in the formation and marched to our assigned spot on the field. When I positioned myself in front of the unit and looked toward the reviewing stand where several rows of military dignitaries and guests stood, I could distinguish our new commander from the taller Lt. Col. Larson. Distance, however, prevented me from forming much of an impression of him.

"Ladies, gentlemen, General Hillard and distinguished guests, welcome to today's ceremony." The narrator's voice boomed through the microphone and across the field. The Change of Command ceremony had begun.

At that moment the sun disappeared, obscured by a fast-moving black cloud behind the reviewing stand. The sky darkened while the Commander of Troops, Major Morris, barked each of his commands and each unit on the field responded on cue and in its turn.

"Battalion!"

"Company!" we all chimed in unison.

"Atten-tion! Receive the report!"

I swiveled toward my unit. "Report!" I snapped.
Each of my squad leaders sounded off "All present!" with a smartly executed salute. During that brief moment, I warned them that we were in for a drowning.

"Stand tall," I reminded them. In turn we sounded off.

I faced the Commander of Troops. "All present and accounted for!"

The dark storm cloud swept over the field, dumping torrents of water, soaking us to the skin through our battle dress uniforms. In true Army fashion, the band played on and the ceremony continued, although those of us on the field could barely hear the rain-garbled words of the commanders, one saying farewell, the other introducing himself. Each time I faced the soldiers, I looked them squarely in the eyes and told them to hang tough. The deluge continued until the Commander of Troops shouted, "Pass in Review!" Then the rain stopped, as suddenly as it had begun.

"Eyes right," I barked when we passed the reviewing stand where our new commanding officer stood. Again, there was no time to catch more than a quick glimpse, but I knew I would meet him personally at the reception following this ceremony.

We were all still dripping wet when we headed for the breezeway for what I thought of as "shake and grin" time. I stood in line to greet the colonel. A slight man with shiny black hair in surprising contrast to his fair skin and pale blue eyes, he struck me as mild-mannered and friendly. His wife, Sandy, seemed friendly, too. She was a petite, pretty redhead with a flashing dimple in one cheek. I learned later that the couple had no children, that a dog and a cat were their only family.

After the reception, Lt. Col. Smith met with his six newly acquired company commanders. Still clad in our wet uniforms, the six of us shivered under the blowing air conditioner while our new boss distributed handouts that included his philosophy of leadership. My first impression was of a quiet, easy-going man in marked contrast to our previous commander. Would he make a good boss? I reserved judgment, for I knew that in the Army, results are what count.

I soon learned that the commander's style got those results. Most of the time he was helpful and patient, able to develop good rapport with his troops. His easy manner, while professional, encouraged people to approach him, and he was always available, willing to help us devise solutions to the challenges of our commands. I found I could talk to him about anything—problems my soldiers or their families were having, my unit's mission, or my career.

He seemed to appreciate me as well, not only for my professional competence but also for my knowledge of the Army installation where we were stationed and its community.

"Is there anyone in Panama you don't know, Captain Fischer?" he asked me at one of the frequent functions we were required to attend.

Obviously there were, but his remark alluded to the solid reputation I'd earned since arriving here in April, 1991, a reputation that rested on more than just my work. I had come to Panama after a decade at installations in northeastern states, and although I had enjoyed my tours there, this tiny tropical country attracted me for a variety of reasons. For an outdoor sportswoman from Texas, the weather, although often steamy hot, was a welcome change from snowy winters. And I felt at home with the Hispanic heritage of the local people. Soon after arriving, I had joined the American Society of the Republic of Panama, an organization in which I met many non-military residents of Panama. The local charitable events we sponsored gave me the opportunity to meet Panamanians and to feel part of the larger community.

My reputation also rested on my involvement in sports. Playing golf brought me into contact with people outside the military, including successful businessmen and politicians. And inside the military, people knew me as the soldier recently selected the top female athlete in U.S. Army South, a region that included Central and South America.

To be fair, I must give Capt. Millie Daniels some of the credit for my accomplishments in athletics. Millie was my best friend in Panama, a tall, dark-skinned woman with a robust, outgoing personality, a veteran of both the Air Force and the Navy. She was the first woman to make the All-Air Force Track Team, and later she was a member of the All-Navy Team and then the All-Army Team. She possessed the ability to bring athletes together, and before I knew what was happening, she'd gotten me hooked on competitive running, a sport I'd neglected since high school days. Often we trained twice a day, first at 6:00 a.m. and then after work at 6:00 p.m.

Over the summer of 1991, we spent several months training for the Army 10 Miler that was to be run in Washington D.C., only to learn that because of a shortage of funds, our local brass didn't plan to send the women's team. Millie swung into action, going all the way to the top—to the general. Not only did we get to Washington D.C., for the Army 10-Miler in October, we wound up taking first place!

I loved competing in running, racquetball, biking, and golf, and Millie loved bragging about my wins. When we were together, she'd introduce me to everyone she knew.

"Hey, do you know Linda? Linda is undefeated in racquetball. She was on the team that took first place at the Army 10-Miler. Last week she took second in a triathlon." And so on. Millie could brag like a mother.

Lt. Col. Smith enjoyed sports, too, I soon discovered, giving us a common interest besides our commitment to the Army and our soldiers. I remember the first time we played racquetball. For all his easy-going ways, he was fiercely competitive, and I'm sure he didn't expect to lose that first game. But he did, and from then on, our games were hard fought and could go either way. Most of the time we played cut-throat (three players) or doubles. Occasionally, when a player didn't show up, the colonel and I would play singles, and I found I had to play my very best to give him a good game.

Sometimes he and Capt. Fry, a short man who hated running, would join me in a run. I was the only serious runner in the bunch, so by the first mile marker, my companions would be soaked, while I seldom broke a sweat.

Jogging along, however, we could talk, and the colonel and I would discuss work or upcoming events.

But fishing was by far our favorite recreation. I will never forget fishing in Panama—the brilliant pink and gold sunrises, the clear green water, the bright blue butterflies swarming along the shore, the orange and black toucans fluttering from tree to tree. And, of course, the fish. Mostly we caught peacock bass, called "sargento" by the Panamanians because the black stripes on their pale green tails looked like sergeants' stripes.

Often we went out in groups, four or five boats trailing each other out from the boat launch, and we always returned from our excursions with fish—and with fishing stories. Stories of the big ones that got away, of casting lines over lines, of hitting stumps (someone had to be "point" on stump patrol), of throwing fish into our buddies' boats when they weren't catching much. Of course, as is usually the case with fish stories, they got better with each telling.

Shortly after Lt. Col. Smith arrived, we learned that he considered himself quite a fisherman, having been stationed previously in Panama and knowing the canal waters well. So naturally we all wanted to impress him with our fishing prowess. I didn't brag about my running, but I *did* consider myself the fisherwoman of Panama, bar none. I could take *anybody* fishing and always catch fish.

I remember how I anticipated that first fishing trip with the new commander and his wife. I'd arranged all the details—getting the boat, the minnows, the food and beverages—everything, and on the appointed day, I motored the couple out to a cove known for its plentiful fish. We fished companionably for several hours, catching some, but not a lot. Suddenly the fish hit the water, splashing excitedly, not more than 20 feet from us.

I yanked the starter cord, and the engine kicked in, but the boat sat stationary, going nowhere. I threw the engine in gear. Nothing. Into reverse. Nothing. I gave it more gas. *Vrrrrrooom!* But the darn boat did not move. In frustration, I pulled up the engine. The propeller was gone! So much for impressing my new boss. We spent the next hour paddling out to the canal where a patrol towed us back to the launch. At the time, I was certain my career was over. Fortunately, I was wrong. In fact, my embarrassing misadventure became another good fishing story for the colonel to tell on future fishing trips, of which there were many.

Notwithstanding the fishing fiasco, I enjoyed a smooth, easy-going relationship with the commander that first year of his command. It was a time of great achievement for the entire MP battalion, with all the units doing well in one way or another. And in the centuries-old military tradition, our success was our commanding officer's success.

I was particularly proud of my unit, designated the best in the battalion. Although at the time I was leading the colonel's smallest company, about 60 soldiers strong, we excelled in several areas. Physical fitness, for example. When the Commander of U.S. Army South issued a challenge for units to strive for excellence in physical fitness and qualify for the Physical Fitness Streamer, we accepted, and our unit ultimately became the only one in our battalion to qualify for the streamer. When we displayed the narrow, brilliant blue streamer on the guidon outside our unit, I felt extremely proud of the soldiers who had earned it.

Meanwhile, inside our unit's barracks, 1st Sgt. Martinez was performing miracles. At the beginning of my command, the barracks' furniture had been in poor condition. But 1st Sgt. Martinez was one savvy soldier, and he looked out for his troops. I recall an incident that illustrates his abilities.

One hot morning (most mornings in Panama were hot), 1st Sgt. Martinez showed up at my office. "Ma'am," he said, "grab your hat and three of those new coffee mugs we just picked up. We need to visit Mr. Torrez."

I grinned, knowing Martinez had something good up his sleeve, picked up the cups and my hat, and took off out the door. On our way across base, he mentioned that he'd seen soldiers unloading new wall lockers over by an adjacent building. Coincidentally, our unit needed new wall lockers.

When we arrived at the scene, Martinez introduced

me to Mr. Torrez, the civilian in charge of all barracks furniture, and I mentioned that we could sure use his assistance. Our furniture was in pretty bad shape, not good enough for dedicated troops, I said. Then I shook Mr. Torrez' hand, presented him with the coffee mugs, and thanked him for how hard his staff worked to take care of our soldiers. What results! Several days later a truck showed up with new wall lockers for our barracks.

This was not an isolated incident, for 1st Sgt. Martinez managed to continue sprucing up the barracks until our unit was the standard bearer for the battalion. We loved hearing that the command sergeant major had ordered the other first sergeants to look at what we were doing and then get their barracks in shape.

Not surprisingly, the unit scored extremely well on the Command Inspections that year. Barracks upkeep was a biggie at these inspections, but each unit's arms room procedures, weapon cleanliness, and training records were checked, also. All in all, I believed the soldiers in my command enjoyed their successes as much as I did. I knew they were America's best, and as I watched how hard they worked, I felt proud to serve with them.

But despite my pride in the unit, I had more goals to reach. In our first meeting, Lt. Col. Smith asked me what I would like to accomplish. "Success in my current command," I told him. "And when I've achieved that, assignment to a subsequent command."

In April of 1993, I attained that goal when the colonel gave me command of a much larger company, with over 200 soldiers. With the additional demands on my time, I worked longer hours, assisted by my new first sergeant, 1st Sgt. Price. Although I believed then that the mutual respect between the colonel and me ran high, in retrospect I can see that our relationship began to change about this time. I was completely unaware, however, that he was experiencing a growing personal attraction to me.

Commanding a larger company wasn't the only added demand on my time. Although I had extended my tour in Panama for a few months to take command of HHC, I had only a year left before being shipped stateside. So I began to spend more time with my close friends, many of them also soldiers who would be leaving Panama soon. My buddy Millie, for example, who was scheduled to leave in November. On our days off, she would often call early in the morning.

"Linda, pack your running clothes and beach stuff. I'll be by in 20 minutes." We might go run in a race somewhere, then head for the beach. Afterwards we would bring her three kids over to my place for a cookout. Fish, of course. Usually delicious, tender peacock bass, always plentiful in my freezer. We'd cook it on the grill, basting it with butter, garlic salt, and a twist of lemon while the kids played in my apartment complex's pool. When the dinner bell rang, they would come running and we'd all chow down. Those were good times.

I wasn't spending time with military friends only. As my tour wound down, I accepted more invitations from civilians who invited me to visit their homes in the valley and on the beaches, giving me an opportunity to see more of the beautiful country I would have to leave soon. So with these changes in my life, I had less time for the commander, and he began to show signs of frustration over my growing unavailability, demanding that I account for time I was not spending with him.

One September day when his office called and urgently requested my presence, sending me racing over to Battalion Headquarters. Closing the door behind him, the commander motioned for me to sit at the small conference table across the room. *Uh, oh,* I thought, *this looks serious.*

"Can you play racquetball with me tomorrow morning?" he asked.

What? For this I left important duties? I checked a miniature calendar in my notebook before telling him I had an appointment scheduled.

He interrupted brusquely. "When I was a commander and my boss said 'Let's play racquetball,' I played racquetball!"

I could certainly understand English, and I was used

to following orders. "What time do you want to play, sir?"

Instead of responding to my question, however, the commander took the conversation in another direction, wondering why I didn't seem to have time anymore to do things with him.

"Because I don't *have* time, sir," I tried to explain.

The next morning we played racquetball, but because I felt coerced, I didn't give him a very good game, which gave him something else to complain about. And so the situation slowly deteriorated. As he increasingly focused his attention on me, I became more resistant. During the months that followed, he grew more demanding and began to command me to be at functions and activities. And my anger grew. I felt like a possession. He made it clear that "no" was not a word he understood or accepted. Then had come that shattering night in his home.

No Escape, No Hiding Place

The telephone's shrill peals awakened me. Still half
asleep, I stumbled to the bathroom to rinse my face. The
phone kept ringing. I yanked a towel off the rack and dried
my face. The ringing didn't stop. When I could bear the
intrusion no longer, I made my way to the living room and
picked up the phone.

"Linda? Linda, Linda, don't hang up. I want to talk
to you." *His* voice.

Memories of the night before and of the horrible
fishing trip earlier in the day crashed over me. My head
pounded, and I felt nauseated, wanting to throw up, but
couldn't because there was nothing in my stomach. I collapsed on the floor, dropping the receiver face up. The walls
moved around me, then closed in.

From the upturned receiver, the colonel's voice
reached into the room.

"Are you there? Linda? Are you there?"

I picked up the phone. "Hello...sir...what?"

His voice went on and on, but I'm not sure I heard
everything. "About the other night...while we were
fishing...Linda?"

With my free hand, I pulled my housecoat tightly
around me. My eyes filled with tears. "No. Not now," I wept.

"But, Linda, I want to talk to you...about us...what
happened...live with myself." His urgent voice filled me
with pain.

"No, I have to go. I don't feel well. Goodbye."

I crawled to the bathroom and braced myself against
the sink, fighting the violent heaving in my stomach.
Through the pounding in my head, I heard the phone shrill
again. On and on and on. I turned on the faucet and bathed
my face in cool water. The phone kept ringing. Finally, in
desperation I pulled the cords from the wall.

Night had fallen by this time, and a cool breeze

wafted through the apartment. I didn't turn on any lights
for somehow I felt safer hidden in the darkness. I stretched
out again on the sofa, pulling a small warm blanket my
grandmother had made over me, and crying silently, drifted
off to sleep.

The next morning, I awoke to the bright sun stream-
ing into the living room. Once again I made my way to the
bathroom. This time my gaze fell on the little pile of clothes
in the corner, the colonel's shorts and T-shirt, that I found
myself wearing when I came home. I grabbed a plastic bag
from the kitchen before I gingerly picked up the clothes,
then stuffed them into the bag like contaminated rags and
dropped them into the trash can.

What should I do next? I didn't want to venture
outside, so I shuffled into my bedroom and slumped on my
bed for a long time, confusion clouding my mind. *I know,
I can call Jim.* I plugged in the phone and dialed the familiar
number in Hawaii where he was currently stationed.

"Hello, you have reached 924-3112. Please leave
your message. Thank you." At the sound of his warm,
cheerful voice, I started to cry, comforted a little even
though I didn't leave a message. What could I say? *Oh, Jim,
I feel so dirty. So unclean.* I wanted to call again, just to
listen to his voice. I wished I knew whether or not he had
returned from the Sinai where his infantry unit was temporarily patrolling the Gaza Strip. *Where are you, Jim?* Sadly
I pulled the cord from the wall.

I took another shower, standing under the water for
a long time, attempting to think rationally about the future.
*What's going to happen? If I report him, who would believe
me? I have to go to work tomorrow. I'll pretend it didn't
happen. I can do this. I can survive.* I washed and washed
and washed, hoping I would feel clean again.

Drying my body brought reminders of *him* touching
me, and I felt sick. *He had no right. He was never supposed
to cross the line. How could he? An Army officer with his
subordinate! Jim, what do I do? Where are you?* I pulled on
a pair of shorts and a T-shirt, my own this time, and wandered around my apartment.

My body was sending hunger signals to my brain, but I couldn't imagine swallowing food. Nothing appealed to me. In the kitchen I grabbed a stack of crackers and poured a glass of water. Then I returned to the living room, put the water and crackers on the table next to me, and slumped on the sofa again and tried to put the pieces of the puzzle together. *The beers. Sandy's absence. My favorite champagne. The condom. Why didn't I see this coming? But why should I have seen it coming? We were MPs. Officers. We did right. For the Corps. We were a cut above. How could I go to work in the morning? How could I face him again?* His violation struck deep to the heart of me. He had no right. Choosing who I wanted to give my body to was the one thing I considered mine. Never the Army's.

Leaving the water and crackers untouched, I stretched out on the sofa, pulled the blanket over me, and slipped into forgetful sleep again.

I woke thrashing, a cold sweat drenching my body, darkness smothering me. I could see him over me, holding me down, that sick grin on his face. I struggled to push him off. *Shhh, Linda. It's a dream. You're home now.*

The sky was dark, and I'd lost all track of time, not knowing what day it was anymore. Saturday? No, Sunday. Sunday evening. *The CQ. Call the CQ, Linda. It's your job. Your responsibility.* In the bedroom, I plugged in the phone and dialed the soldier who was on duty when the rest of us were out of the office.

A clipped but polite voice answered my call. "Sergeant Blaine. How can I help you?"

"This is Captain Fischer, Sergeant Blaine. How are things going?"

"Ma'am, we have no incidents to report. However, the colonel was here looking for you."

"Thanks," I managed to force through my lips. "Have a good evening, Sergeant Blaine."

I'd hardly replaced the phone in the receiver before it rang again. I stared at the beige instrument on my dresser as if it were a dangerous animal. But perhaps 1ˢᵗ Sgt. Price was calling, wondering why I had been out of touch for so long. Normally I checked in often. I picked up the phone reluctantly.

"I've been trying to reach you all day," the colonel's voice boomed. "They said you weren't at the office today. I want to talk to you, Linda."

"Sir, there is nothing for us to talk about."

Make him go away, please.

"I want to know how you feel, Linda."

"Sir, you have no right to ask that question."

He had no right!

"Linda, if I thought you didn't want for that to happen, I could not live with myself."

"Sir, you were way out of line and it will never happen again." *Never!*

"But I need to know how you feel, Linda. I fell in love with…"

Stop him now! "Sir, you have no right to know how I feel or to ask these questions and say these things."

"That means you don't love me?"

"No, sir, I did not say that. I said you had no right to ask me these questions." *Now please go away!*

"That means you *do* love me."

How dare he? "No, sir, I did not say that, I said you had no business asking these questions."

"Linda, I just have to talk to you. I couldn't live with myself if…"

I found the strength to end the conversation. "Sir, that's all. I can't talk about this anymore. Goodbye."

"Okay, Linda, good night."

Good night? How could he imagine I would have a good night? At the time, I didn't realize that for more than a year to come, most of my nights would be haunted by a terrible recurring dream of his assault.

Somehow I managed to get through the following day without seeing the colonel, skipping PT (physical training) in case he might be there. But 1st Sgt. Price seemed to sense something was wrong. His round face creased with concern when he told me that the colonel had been looking for me earlier.

"I told him you were sick," he said.

I nodded gratefully. All day—an eternity in slow motion—I busied myself with paperwork. Late in the afternoon, 1ˢᵗ Sgt. Price stopped in my office again and asked if I would be at PT the next morning.

"No," I said. "And if the commander comes by, tell him I'm sick again."

"Yes, ma'am. And you get some rest. You look real tired."

His kindness almost brought me to tears, and I left the building quickly, determined that no one would see me cry. *Soldiers never cry. No one can know. They wouldn't believe me, anyway.* I drove home in a daze, unaware of the heavy traffic around me.

That evening I stripped off my uniform as if it were on fire and stepped into the shower, letting cool endless streams rush over my body. Afterwards I pulled on some old blue jeans and an oversized shirt. The sun was sinking, and I lowered myself to the sofa, watching the last bright rays fade in the darkness. I longed for the sound of Jim's voice, for more than his message on the machine, and I wished desperately that Millie hadn't left Panama. I felt so alone. *No one to turn to. Where do I go? Who can I trust? I feel so ashamed. So dirty. No one will believe me. I can survive this. Just dig my heels in.*

The hateful phone screeched, making me jump. I wished I could leave it unplugged all the time, but my soldiers needed to be able to reach me. I sucked in a deep breath for courage.

"Hello, Linda? Are you there?" The colonel's voice was like a knife cutting into my soul.

"Sir...what...why must you call?"

"I want to talk to you. Can I meet you? Linda?"

"Noooo!" I screeched. "That is not going to happen."

"Linda, I want you to come to the house where we can talk."

To the house? "No way! Where's Sandy? Where was she Friday?"

"She's in San Antonio for a medical appointment."

"Why didn't you tell us at the staff meeting as in the past that she was gone?"

'I...ah...I swear, Linda, I never planned for it to happen."

Here in my apartment with no one watching, I didn't need to stop the tears from falling or the anger from heating my face. "You have to stop calling here, sir."

"I want to talk to you. Tell me how you feel, Linda."

"You have no right!" I cried, slamming down the phone.

When would the phone calls stop? How much more could I take?

The Nightmare Continues

Although the commander's badgering phone calls tapered off when his wife, Sandy, returned from San Antonio, the harassment didn't stop. Instead the battlefield moved to the workplace where he could call or visit me without his wife's knowledge.

I remember one afternoon when he summoned me to his office. I obeyed with the reluctance I always felt now, never knowing what to expect. He directed me to one of the wooden chairs across from his desk, then sat next to me, only a low end table separating us.

"Linda, I have asked you over and over to share your feelings with me." His voice was low and quiet.

I gazed out the window behind him, not really seeing the softball fields on the other side of the glass, but wishing that I could be far away. That I could be running alone, outside in the hot sun, working off the tension that constantly tied my stomach in knots.

When I didn't respond, the commander continued. "The only reason you have this command is because I got it for you. Colonel Mitchell didn't want to give you a second command. He doesn't think very highly of you, but I went on the carpet for you, Linda. Now you don't seem to show any appreciation for what I've done for you. Just remember you have a board coming up, and my recommendation to Colonel Mitchell will make or break you." He paused. "One more thing, if you are thinking of telling anyone, don't be foolish. No one will believe you."

I didn't doubt his last sentence for a minute, and I felt empty and somehow numb inside, as if everything that made me a person had been ripped away.

"Is that all, sir?" I asked in a whisper.

"Yes, that is all."

I ran from the building, then slowed to a walk and rested on a bench under a pavilion near the softball fields. Today was the first time I'd heard that Colonel Mitchell, my

boss's commander and a man I liked and respected, had
questioned my ability to run a larger unit. But had he really
disapproved of my performance? I wasn't sure I could
believe Lt. Col. Smith about anything anymore.

I told myself to hang tough. The board mentioned
by the commander was the process the Army uses to consider officers for promotion. I was coming up for major, the
rank I'd set my sights on attaining ever since making captain
in 1988. And in the Army, if you aren't promoted, you're
out. I felt trapped. The way my relationship with the commander was going, what chance did I have? In truth, he
could easily destroy my career. *Who can I trust? Who can I
tell my story to? No one. I trusted the colonel, confided in
him. And he has betrayed me.*

During the dark months that followed, I carried my
dirty secret with a heavy heart. In the daylight, I could
almost pretend the assault had never happened, but at night
my unconscious mind refused to deny the truth which
returned to me in terrible nightmares.

I tried to use my running to exorcise these nightmares, thinking *if I wear myself out, if I run to exhaustion,
I'll be able to sleep without dreaming.* So almost every
evening, I would run before heading home. I'd charge down
the sidewalks at a blistering pace as if I were being chased
by demons, anger and pain fueling me. Only when the last
rays of light disappeared would I return home. I would take
a long hot shower to soothe my tired muscles, and then I'd
crawl into bed, trying to focus on happy thoughts—special
moments with Jim, family, friends. And I'd pray for deep,
dreamless sleep.

But almost every night, the nightmare would come.
*I'm standing at a table with a group of people. A banquet is
about to start. I have a smile on my face, although I don't
know any of the people milling around me or why we're all
here. I only know I'm supposed to be here.*

*The main entrance to the banquet room is on the
other side of the room, a score of tables away. I look at the
entrance and see Lt. Col. Smith. I feel the smile leave my
face and chilly terror creep into my bones. I want to escape.
I back away from the table, hoping he hasn't seen me. I see*

*people coming in through a small door at the back of the
room, and I head in that direction, grabbing chair backs to
steady myself. It's as if I can't walk; I'm stumbling. When I
reach the door, I look over my shoulder and catch his pale
blue eyes following me. He starts walking toward me, and I
run out the door.*

*Now I'm outside, people all around me, like a
carnival. I run around looking for a place to hide. When I
see a telephone booth, I slip inside, hoping that he won't see
me. I crouch down, but I can still see him. He's about fifty
feet away and I think he's going to walk away, but then a
couple comes up to the phone booth. They're startled when
they see me crouching down and they pull the door shut. Oh,
God, that turns on the booth light which catches the
commander's attention.*

*I bolt from the booth and head toward a nearby
building. I run inside and it's a hotel lobby. I run to the other
side of the lobby and stop in front of elevator doors. The
door of the center elevator opens. Sandy Smith steps out.
She recognizes me. "Linda, we must hurry or we'll be late
for the banquet." I can't speak. I turn and run into a hallway
which feels like a maze. I can't find my way out. Each time I
turn a corner, I look over my shoulder and the commander is
there at the other end of the hallway. I'm running, running
as fast as I can. He doesn't seem to be running. He's walking, but he still appears at the end of every hallway.*

*I keep running—into total darkness. Then a dim
light appears around me. I'm lying on my back. On a bed, I
think. I'm cold. My clothes are gone. When my eyes focus, I
see those pale blue eyes. I feel his hands on my wrists as he
pins me down. I struggle but I can't get free. I see his sick
grin. I hear "You don't know how long I've been waiting to
do this."*

Then I would wake up, throwing off the covers and
crying, "No!" For the rest of the night, I would fight sleep,
often getting up to prowl my apartment. I'd study, do
paperwork, watch TV, anything to stay awake. Eventually,
however, sleep would overtake me, and again the dreams
would come. By the time morning arrived, I'd be exhausted.

But then I would clench my jaw, determined to stick

it out. *I can survive this. Just a few more months here in
Panama.* Unfortunately, I didn't do a very good job of
convincing myself. I left my apartment later and later every
morning, because I dreaded going to what I now considered
enemy territory. In fact, I rarely even set my alarm any
more, so that if I finally fell into a dreamless sleep when
morning approached, I could get at least a little rest. But no
matter when I arrived at work, I would be exhausted. Often
I'd hear that the colonel had dropped by my office, asking
"Where's the commander?" Then I might find a note telling
me to come to his office or to call.

I remember one particularly tough week. 1ˢᵗ Sgt.
Price was out of the office, taking an air assault course, and
my operations sergeant, Sergeant First Class Lewis, had
stepped in as Acting First Sergeant. Our experienced platoon
sergeant was attending classes in the States, so a new,
inexperienced soldier was filling his position. We were
managing but were stretched pretty thin.

One morning Sgt. 1ˢᵗ Class Lewis greeted me with
the news that the commander wanted to see me ASAP.

"Okay," I said. Then, hopefully, "Is there anything
I need to take care of here before I go?"

"No, ma'am," he responded in his clipped, professional manner.

In no hurry for what I supposed would be another
uncomfortable confrontation, I chose to walk the short mile
to battalion headquarters rather than drive, but I couldn't
postpone the inevitable forever. Soon I was sitting at the
small conference table, nervously watching the commander
across from me. He held some manila folders, and I wondered, what now?

"I want to move your Operations Sergeant, to the
401ˢᵗ MP Company," he said. "He needs experience with a
combat support unit."

I exhaled in relief. "Okay." I had no problem with
the move. Until the commander told me Lewis would
transfer the following Monday. I pushed back my chair
abruptly and stood.

"Monday is not a good time for that kind of move,

sir," I said. "The First Sergeant won't be back for another week, and right now, Lewis is the glue holding the place together."

"I've made the decision, and it stands. Monday he moves." His eyes were icy.

"That sucks!" I blurted in disbelief.

"I don't like your tone, Captain!"

"Sorry, sir, no disrespect intended, but I do not believe it's a good move at this time." I hoped a more conciliatory approach would change his mind.

It didn't. "Apology accepted. I've made my decision, Captain."

"Is that all, sir?"

A curt nod dismissed me, and I strode from his office, so enraged I'm surprised flames of fire weren't trailing me. I do know I slammed the door of the headquarters entrance as hard as I could.

Back in my office, I dropped into my chair. When I looked up, I saw the commander, who must have been following me closely, standing in the doorway. He closed my door and barked, "I don't like the way you talked to me in my office. You were disrespectful!"

I didn't argue. "Sir, there was no disrespect intended. I apologized, you accepted that apology. I just don't agree with the timing of your decision."

"Well, apology accepted, but don't let it happen again!"

"Yes, sir."

I shut the door behind the commander and returned, still fuming, to the mountain of paperwork on my desk. But before I had signed my name more than two or three times, the phone rang.

"Captain Fischer, I called SJA, and they said I could charge you with disrespect," the commander said.

I blinked in shock. The Staff Judge Advocate handles the military's legal problems. I could not believe it. The man who had assaulted me in defiance of clear Army regulations against such behavior had complained to SJA about *me*.

"Are you going to charge me?" I fired at him. "Go ahead. Let's go right now! I'll meet you there. I'm sure we can find plenty more to talk about."

A heavy silence stretched between us until the commander finally said. "No, I'm not going to charge you. I just wanted you to know I could." A reminder I certainly did not need, for I knew only too well that he held all the power and absolute control over my future.

"I apologized in your office, sir. Then I apologized here at my office. I said I was sorry, sir, no disrespect intended."

"Okay, apology accepted."

My hand shook as I replaced the receiver, and tears rolled down my cheeks. Who could I call? I felt like I was losing it. Could I be heading for some kind of breakdown?

I dialed the number of Master Sergeant Martinez, my previous first sergeant. Although of course I hadn't told him about the assault, we'd always been close. All I had to do was ask, and within minutes, his old blue Pontiac sedan pulled up outside my office.

He peered into my face as I climbed into the car. "Ma'am, are you okay?"

"I need to get away from the office, from the commander. He's riding me pretty hard. I just can't take it anymore." How I wished I could tell him the truth. How I wished I could tell *someone* the truth!

"Come on, ma'am," he encouraged me. 'You're tough. You're doing so well in command, and your tour in Panama is almost done. Soon you'll be out of here. In the meantime, is there anything I can do for you?"

"No, Sergeant Martinez," I said. "I just needed a little reassurance."

We drove around for several hours, through the crowded streets of Panama City, into the quieter streets lined with palm trees, down past the canal. Not until after 6:00 p.m., when I felt confident the commander would have left for the day, did I ask Master Sgt. Martinez to take me back. But my heart sank when I found a note in my office. The commander wanted me to stop by his house on my way home.

More Trouble

A spectacular sunset painted the evening sky by the time I pulled into the colonel's driveway, but I had stopped appreciating Panama sunsets. Now I sat stalling in my Chevy, unwilling to approach the house. Just then Sandy descended the home's front steps, followed by her husband, and I stepped out of the car. Although initially Sandy had been friendly to me, lately our conversations had seemed short and stilted. I was certain she didn't know the truth, but she must have sensed the hostility between the colonel and me. She threw me a friendly wave, however, and headed off to the softball fields where a battalion team was playing.

The commander halted on the bottom step, motioned for me to follow him, and turned to walk back into the house.

"Sir," I stood rooted in the driveway and raised my voice. "If you want to talk, we can talk right out here. I'll not go into your house unescorted." *I won't make the same mistake twice!*

He shrugged and motioned me to follow him to the old patio set under the house. We sat across from each other.

"Linda, I'm concerned about the trouble we are having," he began. "I just want to know how you feel."

I groaned inwardly. *Here it comes again. The same endless questions that I will continue to refuse to answer.*

I tried to cut him off. "Sir, I thought you said we would not talk about this anymore. Is there something about the unit you want to discuss?"

"We just don't seem to be getting along. If you could just tell me what the problem is."

My anger boiled closer to the surface, and I bolted from my seat, slamming my open hand on the wooden table top. "*You're* the problem," I shouted at him. "You just don't know when to quit. Leave me alone! And don't ever, ever call me at home any more!"

He started to speak, but I raised my hand. "If you don't lay off, you can find yourself another commander. I can't take much more of this."

I marched to my car. When I pulled away, he stood in the driveway glaring after me, hands on his hips, and I wondered how I would pay for my angry words.

The next day, following another fitful night, I waited until after lunch to go to the office where I found my inbox overflowing with papers to be reviewed and signed. I was struggling to concentrate when Sgt. 1st Class Lewis poked his head into the office.

"Ma'am, just a reminder that we have the battalion run tomorrow. Show time is 0545 hours."

"Thanks for the heads up, Sergeant Lewis," I said. "Well, I guess it's your last day with us. I wish you the best of luck. Are you ready?"

The sergeant lowered his eyes. "Not really, ma'am. It would have been better if my transfer could have waited a week."

"Well, Sergeant Lewis, sometimes it's just out of our hands."

Which pretty much sums up how I felt about my whole life at that time. *Out of my hands. No control.* I pushed papers around my desk for a little longer, but I needed sleep desperately.

I drove to the home of Dan and Julie Knight, my sponsor family in Panama. Every soldier living downtown was required to have a sponsor family on base, and I'd hit it off with Dan and Julie immediately. Both civilians, they lived on base with their four great kids because Dan taught at the military school and Julie worked for the Morale Welfare and Recreation Department. Julie, a tall woman with a motherly figure and face, was fixing a sandwich for lunch.

"Linda, what's up, girl? Want something to eat?"

"That would be great," I said quietly.

"So how are you?" She slapped two more slices of bread on the counter.

"Fine."

She searched my face with her soft blue gaze.

"I don't know, Linda. The kids say you've stopped by for a lot of power naps lately. And I've never seen you like this, so tired all the time. What's going on?"

I knew she wouldn't stop probing until I told her *something*. "It's my boss, Julie. He's been giving me a hard time. He just won't quit."

Her hands stilled. "Linda, has he done something to you?"

Oh, God, she was too perceptive. I stared at the floor, unwilling to meet her eyes. "No. He just treats me like a possession."

"Can you report him?" she asked.

At that moment, I was terribly tempted to blurt out the whole story, but I checked myself. If I told this good friend, she would insist I report the assault, and then I would have to watch my career go down in flames.

I forced words through my lips. "It's one-on-one incidents, Julie. I really don't think anything can be done."

Hiding my secret from someone who truly cared about me took its toll, and I was exhausted by the time we finished lunch. When Julie went back to work, I climbed to the second floor to take a nap in the girls' room. Here, on a twin bed decorated with a flowered bedspread and fluffy white pillows, I could feel safe. And I could sleep, at least until the children came home from school in an hour, and know that I wouldn't be interrupted by harassing phone calls or visits. Then I'd go back to the office and tackle my paperwork.

The next morning the sky was dark when my troops started their run. But before long, the brutal tropical sun rose high in the sky, dropping runners to the ground. We sent soldiers to sick call in record numbers that day.

After the run, the colonel gathered his company commanders for his regular evaluation session. He expressed concerns about the number of soldiers falling out, telling us to lengthen our individual company training runs. And he commented on which company ran the best, made the most noise, and so on—typical comments after a battalion run. Then he asked me to stay after the others left.

I could feel my entire body tense, my breath come shorter. I wondered what was up. More questions about how I was feeling? Or specific criticism about the run?

What I never expected was a tirade about the necklace I wore, a solid gold Spanish coin on a thin chain. Several months earlier, the commander had ordered that no gold necklaces could be worn with uniforms. During today's run, he had spotted my chain working its way free from under my shirt. Now, his face set in an angry scowl, he ordered me to report to his office at 0800 sharp.

I should have known the necklace would get me in trouble eventually. It had been a Christmas gift from Tom, a special forces officer, fellow runner, and good friend for whom I had no romantic feelings whatsoever. When I gave him a T-shirt for Christmas, he called and said, "I'm no good at picking out presents, Linda, so promise me you'll pick out something you like and charge it to me."

I argued for awhile, but Tom insisted. One day I escorted Lt. Col. Smith to Reprosas, a jewelry store in Panama City, to pick up a gift for his wife. He watched me select the gold necklace and ask the sales clerk to hold it for Tom. It was after seeing me wear that pendant that the commander issued his "no gold necklaces with uniforms" order.

At 0800 I stood tall in front of the commander's desk.

"Captain Fisher, I'll not have you disobeying my orders. You constantly challenge me and my authority. Do you understand, Captain Fischer?

"Yes, sir."

"Do you have anything to say, Captain?"

"Sir, I simply forgot to remove the necklace. There was no intent to disobey your order." Probably I should have stopped at this point. "I think you are overreacting, sir. Wearing necklaces was not a problem before. Why now?"

I'd asked, but I tried not to hear the answer. "Because *I* wanted to get something for you. I wanted you to pick out something that *I* could get you. But you didn't want anything else. It drives me crazy."

What could I say? "I'll do my best not to let it happen again, sir. May I go, sir?"

Later that morning Command Sergeant Major Johnson poked his head in my door. "Ma'am, can you talk?"

In the Army, the command sergeant major is the highest ranking enlisted soldier in a battalion, working closely with his or her commissioned counterpart—Lt. Col. Smith in this case. I knew Command Sgt. Maj. Johnson to be a tough but fair soldier, but the big rangy man seated across from me now had trouble meeting my eyes.

"Captain Fischer, I don't know why you and the commander are not getting along. Sometimes when you disagree with the commander, I'd say you're borderline disrespectful. He was very upset when he saw the gold necklace around your neck. When I went into his office this morning, he was fuming and saying that you were constantly challenging his authority, that you disobeyed his order. Ma'am, I'm afraid for you. I've never seen the commander like this, and I don't want to see you get hurt. You *have* to get along with the commander."

Tears sprang to my eyes. I knew that I *did* challenge the colonel's authority and that on occasion I *had* been borderline disrespectful. And I couldn't tell anyone why. All the anger and hurt from the assault and the ongoing harassment was building inside of me, exploding in behaviors that until now had been unfamiliar to me. I know now that I was acting out deep frustration, almost *wanting* something to happen, someone to hear beneath my surface words, but I wouldn't tell. I *couldn't* tell. My career meant too much to me.

I fought back tears while I told the command sergeant major I would do my best to get along with the commander. And so for the rest of my tour in Panama, I never wore that necklace again in uniform, although it often graced my civilian clothes. I wear it still today.

Farewell to Panama

Master Sgt. Martinez, Command Sgt. Maj. Johnson and my friend Julie Knight weren't the only people who noticed a difference in me during my last months in Panama. All my life I'd been fiercely competitive, but I'd also been friendly and outgoing with a sense of humor. Now, exhausted from lack of sleep and stressed by the anger and confusion I hid inside, I found myself losing focus at work and occasionally losing my temper, too. But the more people questioned the changes in my personality and behavior, the deeper I tried to bury my secret.

I remember one day when the Post Inspector General stopped by for a visit. The Office of the Inspector General handled inspections and non-criminal investigations and inquiries, and I really liked the current title holder. A middle-aged guy who was almost completely bald, he rode around the post on his bicycle, checking in with company commanders and offering his services. Usually I greeted him with a warm smile and invited him to sit down for a friendly chat, but today my smile was missing. I wondered if he sensed my uneasiness when he seated himself across from me.

"Captain Fischer, how are you doing?"

"Fine, sir," I replied hesitantly. *Why is he here? Does he know something? Did someone call him? He knows something is wrong, I can tell.*

"How is the unit doing?" he asked.

"Fine, sir."

He let his gaze wander around my office, as if trying to make it easier for me to open up. "I stopped and talked to a few of your soldiers yesterday at the hospital. They were very professional and looked sharp."

"Thank you, sir." I felt sick to my stomach from shoving down the anger and turmoil inside.

Then he turned, fixed my eyes with his faded green

ones, and asked his question again. "How are *you* doing, Captain Fischer?"

I didn't dare answer for a minute, afraid my voice would crack. "Sir, I'm doing fine,"

I said, concentrating on the floor.

He shifted in his chair, obviously unsatisfied with my answer. "Are you sure?"

"Yes, sir." I gulped in air. Anger and hurt threatened to strangle me, and I was afraid I couldn't hold my feelings in much longer.

He rose from his chair. "Well, then, Captain Fischer, I'll be off."

I walked him to the door, hanging tough until he was out of sight before collapsing in my chair. *Should I have told him? But he wouldn't believe me. No one will believe me. And my career will be over.*

The closest I came during that long, miserable spring to breaking my silence came one sunny afternoon. Although the commander had told me that his boss didn't think well of me, I had never lost my respect for Col. Mitchell. The son and grandson of distinguished military officers, he seemed to epitomize the kind of integrity one would expect in a commander.

One afternoon after a particularly difficult week, I found myself standing outside Col. Mitchell's office in Brigade Headquarters. I hadn't thought through exactly what I would say, but desperation had driven me to his doorway.

Col. Mitchell was rising from his desk, collecting a couple of files, when he saw me. "Hello, Captain Fischer. Do we have an appointment right now?"

"No, sir." *What should I say? Will he believe me?*

"I'm sorry, but I'm on my way out to a meeting. Do come back though," he said with a smile as he moved past me into the hall. "Better make an appointment first."

"Yes, sir."

I watched him stride rapidly away from me, and my mind filled once more with conflicting thoughts. *Could I really tell? Would he believe me? Or would he stand behind his male officers and watch my career crumble? I'd better keep my mouth shut.* I still did not realize that sometimes not even a career is worth the internal price you pay for silence. And so I continued to keep my secret, although I knew that some of my friends had begun to notice the colonel's strange behavior.

Every spring we held a carnival and invited military families and local people to three days of festivities. Each company ran a booth to raise money for unit funds. The year before, I'd been in charge of the dunking booth, and when I was the "dunkee," I had persuaded most people to spend a couple of dollars at our booth. This year our unit was managing the ring toss. Not the most exciting booth at the carnival, perhaps, but easy to run and at least I didn't have to get wet!

One evening, after my shift at the ring toss booth, I met a couple of guys—Lance and his friend George—for dinner. We checked out all the food stands before we moved in for the kill, filling our plates to overflowing. Then we found seats at one of the picnic tables in the carnival area. Lance and I had golfed in many a tournament together during the last three years, and we teased each other about missed holes and wild swings while we ate.

I was in the middle of one of my favorite golf stories when Lance's eyes moved to a point over my shoulder. "Isn't that your boss over there?" he asked.

I turned to see the commander standing some yards away. "Why, yes, it is." *Oh, please, must we talk about him just when I'm feeling relaxed and having fun?*

"He sure is a strange one," Lance said. "Last month at that banquet he must have seen us talking because he came over and asked me how I knew you. He asked a bunch of questions in a way that made me feel like I was being interrogated. And since we've been sitting here, he's been circling around and staring like a jealous boyfriend. What's his problem?"

My first instinct was to flee, to escape to my car. But outside the bright lights of the carnival, the night was dark.

"Will you walk me to my car?" I asked Lance,

avoiding his question.

He laughed. "Why? You afraid you might get mugged?"

I couldn't manage a laugh back. "You never know what will happen these days."

My friend must have sensed my deep discomfort, because his laughter stilled and he laid his arm across my shoulder. "I'd be happy to walk you to your car."

He accompanied me across the fields and into the darkness. Even if the commander were lurking near my car, I knew I was safe as long as someone was with me.

Master Sgt. Martinez also provided protection, although I don't know if he realized how much I relied on him. My tour in Panama was winding down and so was the commander's, which meant all sorts of lunches and parties and dinners to attend. Fortunately, Master Sgt. Martinez was invited to most of them. When he wasn't, I invited him myself, for he seemed able to deflect the commander's attention from me.

I remember one evening in particular. Master Sgt. Martinez had long promised to host a special Mexican dinner, so he could show off his wife Norma's exceptional cooking talent. He made good on his promise shortly before I left Panama, inviting five guests to this dinner: the commander and Sandy, Command Sgt. Maj. Johnson and his wife Carol, and me.

I arrived at the Martinez home early that evening. Their youngest son was less than a year old at the time, so Norma needed a little extra help. Fortunately, the baby fell asleep before the other guests arrived, and the three of us sat outside on the back porch, enjoying the cool evening breeze and sipping Norma's famous margaritas. We talked of our time together as first sergeant and commander. I would always see those days as "before." Now I lived in "after."

When we caught sight of the two couples—the commander and his wife, the command sergeant major and his wife—walking toward the house, I blurted to Master Sgt. Martinez. "Promise you will not let me leave until the commander has gone."

"No problem, ma'am," he promised.

Dinner went well. I helped with the baby, who—as babies will—had woken at a most inconvenient time, and Master Sgt. Martinez kept the commander out of my hair. I was feeling confident that I had escaped any possible trouble when Command Sgt. Johnson rose to his feet.

"Thank you for a super evening and a great meal," he said to his hosts. Then to the commander, "Well, sir, shall we head back over to my place?" At his words, Sandy and Carol stood and collected their purses.

The commander, however, remained seated, smiling politely. "You three go ahead. I'll be over soon."

What now? I panicked, my stomach leaping to my throat, when Master Sgt. Martinez and Norma disappeared into the kitchen. Fortunately, the sergeant returned almost immediately to say goodbye to his three guests as they headed out the door. Unfortunately, however, the colonel seemed to be planted in the Martinez living room.

Master Sgt. Martinez came to the rescue. "Sir, there's something I want to show you out here." He motioned toward the back door and led the commander outside.

At that moment Norma stepped out of the kitchen. "Captain Fischer, could you give me a hand? Could you hold the baby while I load the dishwasher?"

I sure could! I never knew what Master Sgt. Martinez showed the commander, but I do know that my boss left before the dishes were done. Then Norma put the baby to bed and the three of us visited in the living room, me feeling relieved and blessed to have the protection of such good friends.

On occasion, the soldiers sheltered me as well from the colonel's unwanted attention, although I'm sure they had no idea of the real reason behind my discomfort. During my final weeks in Panama, our unit spent much of its time preparing for the upcoming Change of Command ceremony that would welcome the officers replacing many of the battalion's commanders, including the colonel and me. This meant I needed to spend a good deal of time in the supply room, as we had to inventory and account for all equipment before the ceremony.

One day I was in the supply room trying to clear up a few discrepancies in the books when the supply sergeant reported that the commander was approaching the building. Weary of my encounters with him, I slipped behind a large gray metal cabinet.

"Tell the commander I'm out of the building," I whispered.

"Have you seen your commander?" the colonel asked when he walked into the room.

The supply sergeant hurried to the counter. "Yes, sir, I saw her leave the building. I believe she went out for a bite to eat."

The commander chatted idly for what seemed like hours while I huddled against the wall, hardly breathing. And there I stayed until after the supply sergeant, who went outside to watch the commander go down the hill on his bicycle, reported that the coast was clear. Afterwards, I could hardly believe I'd actually hidden from my boss.

"Thanks for helping me out today," I said to the soldiers in the room. "I just could not face the commander today."

And so the last few months in Panama crept by while I kept my distance from the commander as much as I could. Avoiding him altogether, especially after work, was almost impossible, however, because of my commitment to my unit's sports events. I had always loved watching sports almost as much as participating, and I particularly enjoyed watching my unit's teams play—basketball, football, softball—because it gave me a chance to see the soldiers in a different light. Some of them loved to brag about "how I won the big game" back in high school, and the older guys told their "back in my day" stories.

The soldiers expected me to attend every game, and I tried hard to meet their expectations—and to give them a little extra incentive to win. During the past rainy football season, the field turned into a huge mud puddle, so I promised that after each win, I would take a belly flop mud slide in which they could join if they wished. After our final win, the whole team lined up beside me, and we turned the mud slide into one more competition, running full speed ahead before flinging ourselves belly down into the mud. I didn't slide the farthest, but the soldiers talked about that day for months afterwards.

Now that spring softball season was here and the fields were dry, the soldiers were trying to think up a new incentive that I could promise them. Our team was doing well, thanks to some powerful sluggers, and today's game would be a critical win for us.

"How about you and the First Sergeant treating us to pizza if we win?" they suggested.

We agreed and then watched our team play the game of their lives. Bases loaded, two outs, winning run at the plate—tension! The lanky soldier cranked the ball out of the field. We won! And we celebrated with pizza, which arrived seconds after the game ended. Actually, the 1st Sgt. and I had ordered pizza long before the final inning. No matter the outcome, we felt the team deserved a reward after such a hard-fought game.

During the game, the commander had kept his distance, thanks to the presence of his wife. But when the last runner stepped across home plate, Sandy headed home across the field. Excited team members invited the commander to share our pizza, which was laid out on the tailgate of a truck. *Wish they hadn't done that! How can I stay out of his way? Just keep moving, Linda. Surround yourself with little groups of celebrating soldiers, but keep him in sight all the time.*

I have pictures of that celebration, and I feel anger and disgust and sadness when I look at them today. The commander has climbed into the back of the truck and sits with his back against the cab. In each picture that includes him, his face is sullen. We've just won a game, yet he is moping as if he's not getting enough attention! The snapshots show me with the soldiers, smiling and patting backs, but my smiles are fixed and phony—sadly different from my normal grin. And I have a beer in my hand, something you never see in my stack of photo albums from earlier years.

I remember watching for an opportunity to escape. When the commander left for a quick trip to the port-a-potty, I said hasty good-byes, ran to my car, and took off. I knew I'd have to do some explaining the next day at work, but I'd discovered I would rather explain later than be trapped.

And then, at last, July 1994. I had only a week left in Panama, and as departing officers often do, I moved from my apartment into the post guest house. Unfortunately, Lt. Col. Smith and his wife, also on their way to a new assignment, were staying there as well. Several nights before my flight, I was preparing for bed when the phone rang. Assuming that a friend was returning a call I'd made earlier, I answered cheerfully, "Hello?"

Shock waves hit me when I recognized the colonel's voice. "Whaaat? Right now, sir? Okay." *He wants to give me my evaluation? Now?*

"Can I come by your room?"

"No, sir!" I barked. "I'll meet you in the lobby."

I took my sweet time getting to the lobby, hoping he would give up waiting for me, but there he stood, folder in hand. While I fought to control the anger rushing through my veins, he actually seemed happy to see me.

"Well, Captain Fischer, I have your report here. I'd like to go over it with you."

We sat down across from each other on uncomfortable lobby couches, but I couldn't seem to focus on his words. As he droned on, I zoned out.

"Do you have any questions, Linda?"

I stood up, reaching for the folder. "No, sir." I took the folder and headed for my room, only to find him following close behind.

"Captain Fischer, could I walk with you?"

I didn't want him near my room, so I led him to a bench outside the front entrance. Although night had fallen, I knew the bright light over the lobby door guaranteed my safety.

"I just want to know how you feel, Linda." Once more I shut out his voice, although I couldn't completely avoid hearing words fade in and out.

"Could you just tell me...your silence...tough on me...fell in love with you that first year...sports...athlete."

I raised my eyes to the night sky decorated with bright stars and a crescent moon and imagined the moment I would escape by plane through that sky.

"Linda, my wife and I had troubles over all this...counseling...she never saw me act this way..."

"I have to go, sir," I said. "I need to finish packing."

He wouldn't give up. "We can still be friends. I'd like to work with you again. It's possible. I could make it happen."

Oh, God, he could. I knew that he had tried to get a job in Texas after I received my orders for San Antonio. My heart raced in my chest. *That must NEVER happen.*

"I *have* to go, sir."

The next morning I rose at 5:00, eager to leave Panama, a country I had once loved. I took a long warm shower, hoping to wash away all the pain, anger, and hurt before I left. I didn't yet understand that my secret would follow me wherever I went, inflicting damage on me and those around me, until I dealt with it.

After I dressed, I phoned down to the front desk to confirm the departure time of the shuttle to the airport. This was one plane I dared not miss, for I didn't want to spend even one more day in Panama. I had learned to travel light over the years, so my luggage consisted of nothing more than one suitcase, a small pull case, and a gym bag, easy to tote down to the lobby. When I discovered the shuttle hadn't arrived yet, I left my belongings at the curb, and returned to the lobby to check out. Then I stepped back outside.

A truck was now parked by the curb—a familiar truck with a boat hooked to the rear end and a dark figure moving out from the side. The commander. What an unwelcome surprise! He insisted on giving me a farewell hug, putting his arms around me while I stood stiff and still, arms at my side. And he reiterated his desire to work with me in the future. Knowing that his connections in the Army might actually allow him to make that happen, I cringed momentarily. But I comforted myself. *That will never happen. This is his last moment to force himself on me.*

The shuttle roared up, the driver loaded my bags, and I left post at last, watching the figure beside the boat disappear in the darkness. During the drive to the airport, the sun rose gloriously as always, but in my anxiousness to be gone, I barely noticed it. At the airport, the lines seemed to move more slowly than I'd ever known them to, and when at last I completed my check-in, I found a seat as close to the boarding door as I could.

Finally, finally, my plane rose into the air, and I breathed deeply in relief. I had escaped! But had I really? Many of my lifelong beliefs about myself, about others, and about the Army had been shattered. And I knew I wasn't the confident, fearless, take-on-any-challenge young woman I'd been before Panama. While the plane winged its way to Texas, I recalled my youth and the days when my fighting spirit was alive and well.

My Fighting Spirit

I was born April 14, 1961, in Biloxi, Mississippi, to a Caucasian soldier, Robert Francis Fischer, and his Mexican wife, Luz Maria. My dad was attending the Air Force's radar school at the time, and when he and my mom couldn't settle on a name for me, his classmates took a vote; I've been Linda Arlene Fischer ever since. My sister Anna was sixteen months old when I was born, and my brother Frank came along four years later.

My father served in the military all my growing-up-years, first in the Air Force, then the Army, so our family moved frequently. In fact, I attended a different school almost every year of grade and high school, so I learned early on how to make friends quickly. Places I remember from those early years include Sumter, South Carolina, and Copperas Cove, Texas.

My dad was—and still is—a handsome man with hair that silvered elegantly when he was still quite young. My mom was younger than he, only seventeen when my older sister was born. Still a kid herself in many ways, she used to grab our hands and dance us around the living room. If my parents argued, I never knew it. So my parents' divorce, when I was in the fourth grade, came as a surprise to me.

We lived in Killeen, Texas, that year, in a house within walking distance of the elementary school. Coming home after school one day, I recognized my grandparents' car in our driveway. Grandma Stephens, my father's mother, and her second husband visited us on occasion, but I hadn't heard anything about this visit, so I felt uneasy. Inside, I found my dad and grandparents in the living room, my sister with them on the sofa, and Frank playing on the floor. Boxes of our belongings—clothes and toys—were piled in one corner. The sad looks on the adults' faces increased my unease. And then Dad told me that my mom was in one of the back bedrooms, waiting to talk to each of us kids individually.

When my turn came, I could tell Mom had been crying. First she told me that I should never forget how much she loved me. Then she said, "Your dad and I aren't getting along, and we won't be living together anymore."

I tried so hard not to cry, but tears leaked from my eyes.

"Your dad is leaving for Vietnam, and you children are all going to stay with Grandma for awhile, so be especially good, " she continued. "Don't drink or smoke or make the mistakes I have made, Linda. Watch what others do and learn from them."

I broke into sobs and hugged her tightly. She left that very day, moving to another small town in Texas, and our father was granted custody of us children. Over the next four years, until her death in a car accident in 1975, our mother visited us occasionally, but we didn't see her on a regular basis. Although I only really knew her for the first ten years of my life, I'll always be grateful to her for giving me life and for the pleasant memories I have of her.

Immediately after the divorce, my father left for Vietnam, and Anna, Frank, and I moved to Alvin, a small town about an hour from Houston, to live with Grandma Stephens. Fortunately, we had always loved our Grandma dearly. We still do.

And how we loved that house of hers! Two leafy pecan trees in the front yard, a huge backyard good for all manner of childhood games, and a sandbox running along one side of the house. Inside we had a nice playroom with toys, books, a piano, and more. None of us ever learned to play the piano, but we loved to hear Aunt Karla and Aunt Irene, my father's sisters, tickle those ivories.

Grandma was, and still is, a short, plump woman with long fair hair that she wraps in thin braids around her head like a crown. She is a loving, caring person who, along with my parents, instilled in me values and beliefs that have stayed with me through the years. She expected us to do our daily chores without complaining. We made our beds, kept our rooms picked up, and every evening Anna and I helped with the dinner dishes. One of my jobs was to clean

George's cage. George was a talkative parrot who could squawk all our names. More than once I came running into the living room, thinking Grandma had called me, only to find George alone in the room, looking very clever. Grandma also took us to Sunday School and church every week, a practice I follow to this day.

A few years ago, our family gathered at Grandma's house in Georgetown, Texas, where she moved to be near my father after his retirement from the military. After Grandma relocated, Aunt Karla moved to Round Rock, a small town near Georgetown, and Uncle Don and his wife moved to Florence, only twenty minutes away. My dad's twin brother Dick and family live in East Texas, so my visits home always feel like family reunions.

We all ate more than we should have for lunch that day and then scattered to relax. I joined Grandma outside on the porch swing.

"That was a great meal, Grandma," I said.

She smiled, "Thanks, Linda."

We rocked quietly for a minute before I began to chuckle as the memories flooded back.

"Grandma, did you know that when we lived in Alvin with you, we were afraid to turn on the light going up the stairs at night?"

"Why, no." She cocked her head, still crowned with those trademark braids.

"Remember how the string that turned on the light hung half way down the stairs? Well, that meant we had to go up half the stairs in the dark before we reached the string. Anna and I would sit at the bottom of the stairs for ages arguing over whose turn it was to make that dash for the string in the dark. Once in awhile, we'd get lucky and Aunt Karla or Aunt Irene would come along and turn on the light for us. But when it was just the two of us, we'd be pretty scared. Whoever's turn it was would scoot up to the string as fast as she could go, yank the string, and scurry back down the steps, trying to escape the boogie man."

By now, Grandma, having obviously not heard this story before, was laughing hard enough to attract other family members to the porch.

"It was doubly scary when you pulled the string and it snapped out of your hand and caught on the top railing," I said. "Then we had to go *all* the way up the stairs to turn on the light!"

After Grandma wiped her eyes, she told one of her own favorite stories. "Well, I'll never forget that day you whipped up on your cousins, Trena and Ricky. Just that morning I'd reminded you to play nice, no fighting. You were swinging by yourself in the backyard, when those two came along. Gosh, you were such a skinny little thing then, Linda. Anyway, Trena sat on the empty swing, so Ricky tried to take yours away from you. You tried so hard to be nice. Finally you gave up and let them have both swings, but they were mad cuz you wouldn't fight. They followed you, and one of them, don't remember which one, shoved you. Well, that did it. You turned around and whipped them both. Then you came running into the house, all out of breath, while they went running off to tattle to their mama. 'Grandma, I'm sorry, I tried to play nice. I didn't mean to fight.' You were so scared you were going to get in trouble. Fortunately I'd seen the whole thing through the kitchen window."

Remembering that day, I laughed until the tears ran down my cheeks. Now the group on the front porch grew larger, and the fishing stories began to circulate. Everyone in my family loves to fish. When we were young, our dad would take us fishing all the time, out in the Gulf of Mexico or on one of Texas' many rivers. We kids carried cane poles with small hooks for wiggly worms on the end of our lines.

The great thing about fishing as kids was that we always caught *something,* even if it was just a tree limb or stump or a rock. Occasionally we even caught a fish, most often tiny sunfish which, at the end of our poles, seemed like the biggest fish in the whole world. When we grew tired of fishing, we'd lob rocks into the water, and we were famous for hitting the exact spot Dad was trying to fish. We never could figure out why that made him so mad, until we became serious about fishing ourselves, of course.

Dad may have yelled when we threw rocks, but most of the time he taught us patiently. He would bait up the hook over and over again, then toss the line out on the end of my pole.

"Okay, Linda, now you have to watch the bobber. When it goes under, pull up on the line."

I concentrated on that bobber until my eyes burned. There, down it went. I had a bite! In my excitement, I yanked on the pole much harder than I needed to, and up flew the bobber followed by a fish. The fish sailed off into the distance while the line whipped around, causing the hook to bury itself in my brother's ear. Of course I thought Frank was scarred for life, and gave up fishing immediately. Well, for that day, anyway.

Not too long after that, Grandma and Grandpa took us on our first fishing trip out on the big ocean. We fished for croakers. To this day I have no clue what a croaker is, but I do know we caught a whole mess of them. And I remember listening in awe to the croaking sound they made when we pulled them out of the water.

On Grandma's Georgetown porch, we asked her to tell us a crabbing story. She was the best crabber in the family. We'd sit beside her at the edge of the pier, checking our lines that had small weights and chicken bones tied at the end. If your line felt heavier, that meant a crab was nibbling at the chicken bone. You pulled up on the line real easy, ever so slo-o-owly, and just when the crab reached the surface, you scooped him up with a net before he could let go. Then you had to transfer the ornery fellow into the cooler.

"Be careful," Grandma always warned. "Those crabs have mean pincers, so grab them from behind."

Boy, was she right! You only had to get pinched once to know how much those pincers could hurt. I always tried to dump the crabs right from the net into the cooler, hoping they wouldn't get tangled in the net.

Grandma started in on one of her favorite crabbing stories. "Remember when I took you kids crabbing one rainy day? When the water was splashing over the pier?

First thing I told you was "Stay away from the edges and stay close to a pole."

I remembered that day well. Grandma was full of good advice, but we didn't always follow it. She turned to remind us one more time to stay away from the...plunk...edges. Oops, it was too late for Frank. Grandma swiftly fished one scared, drenched little boy out of the water. He was none the worse for his dunking, but he stayed close by her side the rest of the day. Not more than an hour later, my sister Anna, older and bolder, wandered to the farthest end of the pier.

"I saw a small wave coming," Grandma reminisced, "but before I could yell a warning, Anna was in the water. Good thing she was a good swimmer and could get herself back on the pier. Before that day was done, believe me, all you little ones was soaked to the bone."

Listening to my family chuckle over our favorite stories, I realized how important those days in Alvin were in shaping my life. For while Grandma loved us and took good care of us, she also had rules. If you disobeyed the rules, you suffered the consequences.

I'll never forget the afternoon Grandma shooed Anna and me outside to play after a rainy morning. "Remember," she reminded us, "don't play by the road. I'm going in to take my nap."

Anna and I played happily enough on the front sidewalk until we noticed a small stream of water running along the side of the road. I'm not sure which of us had the bright idea to float sticks in the stream, but before long we were building dams with pecans and rocks, challenging each other to floating stick races, and laughing loudly.

"Having a good time?" All of a sudden Grandma was standing over us.

Still laughing, we said, "Oh, yes, Grandma."

Then we raised our eyes to the hands planted firmly on her hips. Uh, oh! We knew we were in trouble now.

"What did I tell you about the road, girls? Now go get a switch off the tree!"

"We're sorry, we didn't mean to play by the road,

that's where the water is, Grandma, we're sorry," we cried in unison.

She just barely touched our little behinds with the weeping willow tree twig, but we hollered like we'd been whipped, hurt more by the thought of being spanked than the reality. That day we surely learned that crossing the street was a big no-no!

During our year in Alvin, a new family with a bunch of kids moved in across the street. We gazed at them wistfully, hopelessly, trying to figure out how we could get to the other side without crossing the street. One evening at dusk we spotted a swarm of light bugs in the new kids' yard. We yelled across the street, trying to explain to our neighbors how to smear lightbugs on your shirt so you would glow in the dark. But they just didn't get it. Was it worth a swat with the willow twig to dash across and help them, we wondered? Finally we got wise. We would ask Grandma's permission! Naturally, the minute we asked, she walked us over.

"Now, you kids stay in the yard and I'll be back for you later," she said.

Catching light bugs is easy, but you have to hold them just right to smear the glowing tails on your shirt. If you're skilled enough, you can even spell your name or make a picture with the smears. I don't remember who taught us the art of light bug smearing, but we all became experts eventually.

Although life in Alvin was great fun, Grandma made sure we didn't neglect our studies. Every day after school we sat at the kitchen table, had a snack, and then did our homework—spelling, reading, and writing—with Grandma, Aunt Karla, and Aunt Irene close by if we needed help. The study habits I learned then stayed with me all my life.

On holidays and birthdays, Grandma made a big fuss over us. At Christmas one year she surprised my sister and me with matching western outfits. Anna and I paraded around in our new pants, shirts, and vests, sure we were the coolest cowgirls in the West. I think my Aunt Dolly, another one of my dad's sisters, made the outfits. She and her family lived on a ranch outside Houston.

On one visit to the ranch, Anna and I put our brother Frank up on a pony called Candy. Frank was a cute little guy, probably about five or six at the time, all big brown eyes and mischievous grin. Dressed in our western outfits, Anna and I were pulling Candy along at a pretty good pace, laughing and jabbering, when we heard Frank hollering. When we looked back, we saw that the saddle had slid underneath the pony, with Frank still hanging on for dear life. We rescued him, of course, but I think that story will live forever in our family's history.

Good as those days in Alvin were, we missed our father. He sent frequent cards, letters, and audio tapes from Vietnam, and I still have the card and letter he sent for my eleventh birthday. I remember how happy we were when he returned safely from the war and how Frank followed him everywhere at first, even keeping his little hand in Dad's back pocket for a time.

After a short leave, Dad moved us all to Georgia where he would be stationed, and I would start the sixth grade. We didn't live there long, just the one year, but that was long enough for me, for I experienced my first taste of racism there.

None of us Fischer kids were shy—we couldn't afford to be—so as soon as we moved into our house, located in an all-white neighborhood, we hurried out to find new playmates. We saw kids about our age playing across the street, but when we went over to introduce ourselves, their parents called them in, and when we knocked on the door, nobody answered. After this happened several times, we asked our dad, "What's wrong with these people? Why don't they answer the door? Why won't they let us play with their kids?"

Dad did the best he could to explain prejudice to his three little part-Hispanic children, but it never made much sense to me. As far as I was concerned, the neighbors were just plain rude! My brother and sister and I crossed the railroad tracks and played with the black kids, who became our good friends. I can't say I understood then what prejudice was all about, but I knew I didn't like it.

I remember hanging out one day in the schoolyard with my two best friends, Barbara, who was black, and Janet, who was white. Three white boys with scowling faces and clenched fists challenged us.

"Hey, where do you think you are going?" one of them squawked at Janet.

"I'm just walking," she replied.

"Well, you can't walk with *them*," another boy said, pointing at Barbara and me.

I couldn't believe it. "Janet, do you have a problem walking with me and Barbara?" I asked my friend.

"Nope," she said defiantly.

That made the boys mad. "You're coming with us!" one of them shouted at Janet, reaching out for her.

"You'll have to walk through me first," I shouted back, stepping in front of Janet. When the boy grabbed my arm, anger surged through me, and I sprang at him and his buddies. I'm not ashamed to admit that I gave it to all three pretty good.

Later, the principal called me to his office. Nervous about the trouble I might be in, I scuttled through the door to see three fingers pointing at me.

"She's the one!" the boys chorused.

The principal, a big black man with a round face, broke into a grin. "Wait outside the office please," he said to me. On a wooden bench outside his office door, I listened to him berate the boys.

"She's only in the sixth grade, no bigger than any of you. I can't believe you would want to tell anyone a little thing like that beat up all three of you. Now get on out of here!"

I grinned, too, while I listened to his scolding, but when the boys skedaddled and the principal called me into his office, I felt scared.

"Tell me what happened out there," he ordered, fixing me with his no-joke dark eyes.

"Sir, I was just standing my ground for what was

right. They were being bullies. My dad and my grandma taught me to always stand up for what is right."

The principal frowned. "You know you are not supposed to fight in school, Linda. You can be expelled."

I thought I might die, right there in the principal's office. Dad would be so angry if I were expelled from school!

"Well, considering the circumstances and the fact that you've had no other incidents, I'll let you go with a warning. Now get back to class."

"Thank you, sir!" Now I was the one skedaddling out of the principal's office. I never noticed those particular boys again, but believe me, I wasn't sad to leave that school at the end of the year.

We moved back to Killeen, Texas, just outside Fort Hood where my father was stationed. We children settled into school and made friends quickly, as we'd always done before. The big event during our two-year stay was my father's remarriage, to Josie Valdez, a pretty lady with a son of her own named Vincent, just about Frank's age. Now we were a family of six. In the seventh grade at the time, I had a few rough spots with my new step-mom. But she's been good for my dad, and we've grown closer over the years. Now when I talk about "my parents," I am definitely including Josie.

During my junior high years in Killeen, I began my life-long involvement in sports, particularly track and field, and I still treasure the bright ribbons I won in sprints and high jump events. Then we were off to Schofield Barracks in Hawaii for two years where I collected more ribbons, this time in track and in swimming.

In 1977, my father retired from the military and moved to Georgetown, Texas, a town not far from Austin. Again I jumped right into school sports. My scrapbooks from the years in junior high and high school are packed with ribbons, certificates, and newspaper clippings about track meets I participated in. But I always kept up my grades, earning a place in the National Honor Society and Rotary Scholar. And beginning the summer of my junior year, I worked, too.

That summer I heard that an electronic assembly company called TESSCO was hiring, and that I should see a man named Mr. Skinner. I hurried over, only to hear from Mr. Skinner that they had all the help they needed.

"I'm available to start on Monday," I said, ignoring his polite brush-off. "I could work in the mornings from 8:00 to 12:00. In the afternoons I run track and cross country, so I would be part time and save you money. I could even work weekends and it won't cost you overtime."

"How old are you?"

"Seventeen. And I can start Monday," I said.

"You have to be eighteen to operate some of the equipment. You're just not old enough."

But I had a solution to that problem, too—a waiver from the school district allowing me to work before I was eighteen.

When I told Mr. Skinner about the waiver, I added, "And I can start on Monday."

"Okay, you can start on Monday," he finally said. So I did, working for his wife Shirley who was one "tuff" lady. But for years, Mr. Skinner remembered me as the girl who wouldn't give up.

Immediately after graduating from high school in 1979, I enrolled at Southwestern University, thanks to Doc, the athletic director of the university who sent me to the admissions office when I was looking for a job. Although I had little money for tuition or expenses, I earned a degree in three years with the help of government loans, grants, and a lot of hard work. There was no time for sports. When I wasn't going to class, studying, or sleeping, I worked—at TESSCO in the summers, at the university bookstore during registration periods, and in Doc's student work program at the school's gym during the academic year. I did find time for some fun, of course, with friends from school and home.

I majored in physical education and was considering a career in coaching, but my dad kept encouraging me to check out the military. I guess he saw me as good Army material because he knew how determined and disciplined I was. Anyway, shortly after graduation, I enlisted in the Army. After a year, I attended Officer Candidate School (OCS) in Fort Benning, Georgia. At OCS I learned that although the Army was demanding, I had the "right stuff," and in August, 1984, I earned my commission as an officer. Soon after, I attended Military Police Officer training, and I've been an MP ever since.

My first assignment was at West Point, New York, where I served with a military police company, primarily responsible for traffic control for the frequent sporting events and ceremonies that take place at the prestigious Army academy there.

After some additional training, I was stationed at Fort Monmouth in New Jersey. Then in 1989, I was assigned to the West Point Prep School, a military school for young men and women to prepare for West Point. I enjoyed helping these young people prepare themselves for their hoped-for military careers, and it was during this time that I took my first command: Commander for Bravo Company.

In April 1991, I arrived in Panama, full of enthusiasm for my new posting and happy about my career in the Army. Because I'd grown up in the military world, I was comfortable not only with the uniform codes and the regimentation, but also with the constant moving. And I thrived on the tough physical demands and competitive atmosphere.

My first two years in Panama were some of the best in my life for many reasons—the weather, the Latin American culture, the close-knit military family, the opportunity to be part of the larger community. I enjoyed the challenge of ever increasing work responsibilities and felt respected by my superiors, my peers, and my subordinates. Sometimes I even found myself helping others outside my direct chain of command.

I recall a situation with a female soldier, Staff Sgt. Gordon, whom I knew through sports competition. When she heard rumors that the MP battalion might release her from the Army, she came to me and shared her concerns, even though she did not report to me.

"I can't promise you anything," I said, "but I'll talk

to the battalion command sergeant major."

Several days later I sat across from Command Sgt. Maj. Johnson, a fair and open-minded man. Never mentioning Staff Sgt. Gordon's name, I talked to him about the concerns of female non-commissioned officers. After all, the situation wasn't *that* different for female commissioned officers, and I knew I had credibility with Command Sgt. Maj. Johnson.

"Women feel they have to prove themselves before getting certain high payoff jobs," I explained, "while men come qualified. And a woman sometimes feels she's in a Catch-22. If she doesn't sleep around, she is labeled a lesbian. If she does, she's considered a whore."

Command Sgt. Maj. Johnson listened carefully while I cautioned him that some women felt they were being judged on their appearance, that being athletic or having a husky build reflected on their sexual preference. He hadn't thought of the woman's perspective, he admitted, and he wanted women to succeed in the Army. When I left his office, I felt he'd been receptive to my suggestions, and I was delighted to hear that after reviewing Staff Sgt. Gordon's case, he transferred her to a position in which she proved successful.

Incidents such as this reinforced my belief that the Army was the right place for me, and I was proud to stand with my fellow soldiers as a great force for justice, protecting our nation. In return, I believed the Army would take care of us, would protect us. Until, that is, the nightmare of my last year in Panama.

The Rage Within

July, 1994. On the plane home from Panama, I
visualized my parents waiting for me at the end of the exit
ramp in Dallas. First, we would enjoy a three-way hug, then
saunter over to the baggage claim, all trying to talk at the
same time. On the way home Dad would tell jokes, some
new and some I'd heard a thousand times. The familiarity of
my family and surroundings would surely wipe away my
bitter memories of the past year.

Mom and Dad were waiting at the end of the exit
ramp, just as I'd known they would be, and we embraced
tightly, me holding on a little longer than usual, not wanting
to let go. On the way home, Dad did tell a couple of jokes,
and we stopped off at a fast-food joint for a bite to eat. How
relieved I felt to be back in the good old U.S. of A. I didn't
even mind the changes to our home in Georgetown. Since
I'd graduated from high school, my folks had added a
bedroom, bathroom, and hot tub. The living room had been
expanded, a dining room added to the side of the house, and
my old bedroom was now office space. But, the house still
felt like *home*—a place I could be safe.

Unfortunately, I found I couldn't revive the old
enthusiastic Linda of previous visits home. Usually I would
dash right out and visit my friends. I would return to the
First Presbyterian Church. I would stop by to see the
coaches and staff out at University Gym, many of them still
there from my college days. And I would drop in at the high
school and catch up with the teachers who had encouraged
me to do my best.

This time, however, I stayed home. I didn't want to
see people who knew me as a *gung ho* career officer.
I wasn't so proud of the Army anymore, and I feared that my
friends would ferret out the reason why. So I hibernated at
home during my two-week leave, resting my weary spirit
and trying unsuccessfully to make sense of the experience in
Panama.

Several days before I left town to report to my next assignment, Betty called. My best friend from high school days, Betty is a spunky, cheerful Hispanic woman with three kids.

"Hey, girl, someone told me you were in town. What's going on?"

What can I say? Normally I would have called on my first day back. "Sorry, I haven't called, Betty. Let's get together in the next couple of days. When are you free?"

She suggested shooting pool at a small local bar that very night, and when she picked me up at 7:00, I was glad to see she hadn't changed and hoped she wouldn't notice that I had. We had a good time catching up on the news, but knowing that I couldn't share *all* my news with her left me exhausted. I prayed that my new assignment at Lackland Air Force Base near San Antonio would bring me some relief from the stress of keeping secrets.

At Lackland, I commanded a small unit of about 30 highly skilled soldiers who trained dog handlers and their dogs from all branches of service. The unit's first sergeant, 1st Sgt. Perez, was a levelheaded, experienced manager, so my job wasn't too demanding. All in all, it was a good working situation. Unfortunately, I couldn't enjoy it as I had hoped. The anger I tried to repress about the assault and harassment in Panama kept escaping, and I found myself exploding at subordinates or even other officers. Any resistance I encountered seemed to provide an opportunity to release this anger, and to my bewilderment, I picked fights with almost anybody, no matter their rank. I looked for any target, lasers up, in the strike position. Me, who had always seen myself as the protector, not the bully.

I remember an incident with the lieutenant colonel who commanded the Air Force unit my soldiers worked with. We were trying to work out a training schedule, and I stood up for my soldiers, arguing that they shouldn't have to stay late after hours. Instead, training should take place during the regular workday.

With the commander and me coming from different points of view, the conversation heated quickly. Eventually

I won the training time for my soldiers, but not until I had ranted and raved in what I recognized later as behavior that was unprofessional and dangerously close to the line.

Another disquieting incident took place at a bowling alley where a group from our office was participating in a fund-raiser. We were having a good enough time attracting the attention of some soldiers in the lane next to us. When, in response to a question, I mentioned that I was an officer, one of the young soldiers innocently remarked, "You couldn't possibly be an officer. You're too pretty."

Without warning, I let loose the anger bottled up inside, leaving the soldier and those around me in shock.

It wasn't that I didn't *try* to control my anger at work. Whenever I arrived at the office in a foul mood, exhausted from fighting off ugly dreams at night, I would avoid my soldiers, not wanting to take my problems out on them. Or I might give them a warning. "Look out, I'm in a bad mood today." Not until I'd spent some time alone in my office conducting an attitude check could I come out and make small talk.

One morning I looked up to see a soldier standing before my desk.

"Ma'am, I've got something for you, but I'm afraid to give it to you," he said, clutching a small brown paper bag to his chest. Then, handing me the bag, "Nah, you have a sense of humor."

Inside I found a coffee mug that pictured a distraught-looking woman and the words, "Be kind, I'm having a bad hair day." I still have that mug, a poignant reminder of too many "bad hair days."

I struggled constantly with the behavior that I knew must puzzle my soldiers, trying to make it up to them in other ways. For the unit's family Christmas party that year, I hired the most real-looking Santa you ever did see, and I'll never forget the pleasure I felt watching my soldiers crowd around that Santa with their kids. Later, I treated the soldiers to a Christmas feast at the officers' club. I truly wanted the best for my unit, and all I can do now is hope I taught them skills that helped them get where they wanted to go. When I look back, I think they knew something was very, very wrong, although I doubt they ever suspected the truth.

As my anger escalated, I became deeply troubled that I couldn't control my outbursts of indiscriminate anger, and I began to avoid my soldiers and others at Lackland whenever possible. I knew my outbursts could very well jeopardize my career, but I never considered seeking help from the Army. *From the Army? Who would believe me over a lieutenant colonel? Deal with it yourself, Linda.*

Sadly, my rage touched my family as well. One afternoon in Georgetown, when my brothers and parents and I were watching football—the Dallas Cowboys, of course. Our family has always loved to tell jokes, and when we get together, we share winners we've heard since our last visits.

Frank told a joke, one I don't even recall anymore. But for some reason, his words triggered the feelings I kept buried so deep, and for a moment I slipped away to another place and time—a place and time I didn't want to remember. I felt scared, and that fear generated anger.

"Well, isn't that the most ignorant thing I've ever heard you say!" I yelled without warning, before storming out of the room and leaving my family to wonder what on earth was wrong with Linda.

Afterwards, of course, I always regretted my outbursts. I loved my family, Frank no less than the others. Because he was littler than me, I'd always tried to protect him, and we'd spent hours together as kids, playing ball or reading or doing whatever he wanted to do.

As children, Frank and I were playing in the yard close to the sidewalk. A boy rode his bike past us, nearly hitting Frank, who was about six at the time. I moved Frank farther away from the sidewalk before asking the biker not to ride so close to my little brother. The bigger boy took my request as a challenge. He pedaled by again, so close this time I stepped out in front of Frank. The bike hit me instead. Protecting Frank, taking care of him, had been my lifelong pattern. Why was I lashing out at him now?

I hated that I couldn't control my anger, that I would strike out at my family and say ugly things. And I knew my parents, my sister and brothers were watching me, wondering what was wrong. One day my dad asked me if everything was okay. I was fine, I assured him, blaming my behavior on overwork or—once again—using the bad hair day excuse. I knew better, of course.

I began to search for a way to control my anger. Not by telling my secret. Never that. But I remembered Jim, years earlier, telling me about sports officiating. He thought I would make a good referee or umpire and recommended that I give it a try. I had passed on that at the time, but now, as I searched for answers, I thought of his words about the importance of staying in control when you are dealing with coaches, players, and fans. Maybe if I began officiating at community sports events, I could regain some of my old self-assurance and emotional stability.

I attended training clinics, where I learned the rules and mechanics and signals I would need, and soon I was officiating at softball and basketball games almost every night of the week. Jim was right; officiating *is* great anger control practice. You have to keep your cool when your every instinct is to lash back at the nasty jibes from coaches and fans. And I found I *could* keep my cool. *So maybe I've conquered this anger thing. Maybe I've finally left Panama behind. Maybe I can get on with my life now.*

How wrong I was.

Breaking the Silence

I sprang out of bed earlier than usual one sunny morning in September, 1994. On this day, the Army was releasing the promotion board results, and I would learn whether I would someday be Major Linda A. Fischer—or an officer washout. I was living in a spacious two-bedroom apartment in San Antonio, considerably nicer than some of my earlier military accommodations, and not far from Lackland AFB, so it wouldn't take me long to get to work. And I knew that the first sergeant would have already heard the results when I arrived. I gulped my orange juice and dashed out the door.

When I walked into the office, 1ˢᵗ Sgt. Perez stood grinning broadly beside a desk covered with donuts and coffee. *Whew!*

"Ma'am, you need to call the head shed," he said, handing me a slip of paper with a scribbled phone number. The head shed was what we called Headquarters. "They have something they want to tell you."

I dialed the number. "Captain Fischer, congratulations," I heard after I identified myself. "You've been selected for promotion to major. Your sequence number is 3271."

To stagger promotions throughout the year, the Army gives you a sequence number. My number meant I would attain the title of major in about eighteen months.

"Thank you, sir." I could feel my own grin splitting my face.

After celebrating over the spread my soldiers had provided, I stepped into my office to call my parents who I knew were eagerly awaiting my call. We enjoyed a short family celebration by long distance, and when I hung up, I relaxed into my chair, still beaming. *One more goal achieved!*

The ring of the phone startled me, and suddenly fear

replaced my elation. When an officer is selected for promotion, friends, colleagues, and current and past superiors
customarily call with their congratulations. *Past superiors?*
I stared at the ringing phone. *Lt. Col. Smith! Don't touch the
phone, Linda!*

I jumped from my chair and hurried down the hall to
another office. "Please see who that is, Sergeant Jones."

The young soldier at the desk complied. "Army
Training Detachment, can I help you?" He paused. "Please
hold. It's Colonel Mitchell, ma'am."

"Put him through," I said on my way out the door
back to my office. In what turned out to be a blessed quirk
of fate, Col. Mitchell, once my commander's boss in
Panama, had also been transferred to Texas and was officially stationed at Fort Sam Houston, thirty minutes away.

"I wanted to be the first to say congratulations on
your selection for promotion," his cheerful voice greeted me.

"Thank you, sir," I said. I had run into Col. Mitchell
several times since our return to Texas, and he was always
so friendly that I had trouble believing he'd ever said
negative things to Lt. Col. Smith about me.

"Laura and I will be calling again. We'd like to take
you to dinner to celebrate."

I replaced the receiver with a sigh of relief. I'd
escaped this time. But I was still convinced that my promotion would give Lt. Col. Smith reason to call, so I ordered all
my calls screened and refused to otherwise answer the
phone. 1ˢᵗ Sgt. Perez raised his bushy eyebrows at my
request, but immediately passed the instructions to the
personnel in the orderly room.

Several weeks after the promotion list was released,
my parents hosted a celebration cookout in Georgetown. My
whole family—sister, two brothers, Grandma and Grandpa
Stephens—would be there. I managed to slip out of the
office a little early that Friday afternoon and arrived home
earlier than expected.

Dad was watching television in the living room and
Mom was in the kitchen when I walked in the door, but they
surrounded me with big hugs the minute they saw me. The

excitement and pride on their faces warmed me.

"Linda, we both want you to know how proud we are of you," Dad said, getting serious on me. "I know it can be tough to be away from your family, moving around. We're glad that you are here and that we can share this with you."

I felt my eyes burn with tears as I struggled with my emotions. "Thanks. You both have been there for me when I was ready to hang up my hat. I appreciate your support."

Mom introduced a more practical subject. "Did you have lunch? Are you hungry?" She was heading back through the swinging doors into the kitchen when she called over her shoulder, "Oh, you have some mail in here."

I followed her into the kitchen to the counter where unopened mail always awaited its owner. A large white envelope lay face-up. *That writing!* My heart began to race, and I could feel the blood rush to my face. *That return address! Lt. Col. Smith!* In less than a second I was transported back to a dark bedroom where iron arms pinned me down. *Danger, here in my own home. Wasn't it enough that he'd invaded my body and my workplace?*

I snatched up the letter and without opening it, tore it into four pieces which I hurled to the kitchen linoleum. *How dare he dirty this house, my family, my home?* Leaving my parents stunned in the kitchen, I grabbed my weekend bag, stormed off to a bedroom, and proceeded to unpack my clothes, flinging them on the bed while I fumed silently.

My father entered the bedroom holding the remnants of the ripped card.

"Linda, what is going on?"

I didn't blame him for the question. Although he'd seen me angry before, I knew my recent behavior puzzled him greatly. But I wasn't ready to share my anger and shame yet.

"This is from someone I have no desire to hear from," I said, and I left it at that.

Despite the weekend's rocky beginning, we managed to celebrate my promotion with no further fireworks, but from the moment I saw that card on my parents' kitchen counter, something changed inside me. I decided that *I* would begin to control the situation, as much as I could. He would not have any more contact with me. And I would not resort to fearful tactics like having my calls screened. Somehow the commander's invasion of my home had awakened the fighting spirit I'd repressed for over a year now.

The following Monday afternoon found me in the office of Col. Sherwin, the Air Force officer I worked for. I had made an appointment as soon as I arrived at work, and the morning hours dragged slowly, as I contemplated the step I was about to take. I wasn't sure exactly what I would do, what I would say, I only knew that things had to change.

I held out the card fragments to Col. Sherwin. "Sir, I was contacted by my previous commander. I'm afraid of this man and I don't want any more contact from him."

The colonel leaned forward. "Can you tell me what happened, Linda?"

"Sir, this man harassed me for over a year. Let me just say things got ugly." In six months, I had not told a living soul about the assault, and now that I was close to opening up, I couldn't go on. My stomach heaved, and my eyes began to tear.

"Sir, I need to go," I said, rising from my chair. *I wish it would go away. The pain, the hurt, the anger. And the fear. How can I talk about it without crying? But soldiers don't cry. Soldiers never cry!*

The colonel seemed reluctant to let me leave. "Linda, here's my phone number. Feel free to call." He thrust a small piece of paper into my trembling hands.

Not trusting myself to speak, I nodded "yes" and fled into the hot sun where the tears came fast. All the way home and then, curled on my couch, I cried and cried.

Lt. Col. Smith's words echoed in my mind. *If you're thinking of telling anyone, don't be foolish. No one will believe you.* He's probably right, I thought. Telling *might* destroy my career. But not telling was destroying my *life*.

I simply could not live like this any longer. I retrieved the slip of paper from my pants pocket and reached for the phone.

"Sir, this is Captain Fischer calling."

"Linda, I'm glad you called." The colonel's voice was warm. "I felt like there was more you wanted to tell me."

Oh, yes, there's more. So much more. "Can I talk to you again tomorrow, sir?"

"Yes, I'll have my secretary call and tell you the time in the morning. In the meantime, I'd like for you to call Chaplain Bennett tonight. Would you do that for me?"

"Yes, sir."

Col. Sherwin must have worried that my affirmative answer was merely a courtesy response, because minutes later Chaplain Tim Bennett called me. We'd met at a staff meeting a week earlier, and I'd been impressed by his cheerful manner.

"Colonel Sherwin called, Linda. It sounds like you have had a rough time. Are you going to be okay tonight? We could meet right now if you need someone to talk to." His obvious compassion flooded through the phone lines.

"No, I'll be fine," I said. I knew I wouldn't be *fine,* of course, but I couldn't imagine that the night ahead could possibly be worse than others I'd survived recently. Predictably, I tossed and turned all night, watching the clock mark every half hour. Tomorrow my secret would be out, and it would be too late to turn back. But I had no intention of turning back. Not since the commander had invaded my home.

When I dragged myself into the office the next morning, I must have looked as bad as I felt.

"Are you okay, ma'am?" 1st Sgt. Perez asked, his face reflecting concern.

I gave a noncommittal nod. *Am I okay? I haven't been okay for a very long time!*

A note from Col. Sherwin's office lay on my desk; he could see me at 1:00 p.m. in his office. I immediately called his secretary.

"Could the colonel meet me in the chapel?" I asked. I doubted I would be able to control my tears during our meeting, and I didn't want to be seen coming from the colonel's office with reddened eyes. Military installations are like small communities in which rumors spread quickly.

That afternoon Col. Sherwin and I sat down across from each other in Chaplain Bennett's office behind the chapel, and for the very first time I told my secret. And yes, sometimes I cried, overwhelmed by feelings of deep shame and rage, as I struggled to find the words to tell the ugly story. After relating the events in Panama, I tried to explain the emotions—the anger and the fear—that had been triggered when I saw the card from Lt. Col. Smith. How that card seemed to represent his foot in the door, forcing his way back into my life.

Col. Sherwin listened quietly, asking questions when my emotions overcame me. When I had said as much as I could, he recommended two courses of action: first, that I tell my story to the Air Force Staff Judge Advocate, and second, that I get counseling. But I didn't need to make any decisions right away, he said.

"Would you stay and talk to Chaplain Bennett?"

When I agreed, the colonel left me alone to recover for a few minutes. I knew my eyes must be swollen and my face blotched from crying and that my ordeal was by no means over. I did, however, feel some relief. It was as if vents had been opened in the volcano inside of me. The lava still flowed, bubbling hot, but the destructive pressure that had threatened to blow me apart had been released.

By the time Chaplain Bennett came in, I was calm— at least on the outside. He asked me if I wanted referrals to professional counseling, and when I told him I was reluctant to go that route, he offered his own assistance, and I gratefully accepted. For some reason, I immediately trusted him, this compassionate man with his shock of red hair and freckled skin. Before I left his office that day, we scheduled several dates to meet, and I attended his church for the rest of my tour at Lackland. I'll always be grateful for his help.

Out in the October sun, I breathed a sigh of relief. I didn't know what lay ahead, but I knew I had taken an important first step. Back in my office, I took the second step. A note from the colonel in charge of the Air Force SJA office recommended that I talk to a Capt. Reynolds on his staff. I called and made an appointment for the following day.

In her office across base, Capt. Reynolds, an Air Force lawyer, outlined several courses of action I could take. Making a formal complaint to her was one. Or I could file a complaint with the Inspector General's office. I listened intently. *But my career! I've seen what happens to officers who file formal complaints. Isn't there another way to handle this?*

"What I want is for this guy to leave me alone," I explained.

Given my reluctance to initiate a formal investigation, Capt. Reynolds recommended a third option. I could hire a civilian lawyer to send the colonel an official notice prohibiting any further contact.

The idea appealed to me. Maybe with a simple legal document, I could frighten the colonel away permanently. So for the next few weeks, I perused the newspaper and yellow pages, searching for just the right law firm. Then one evening the local TV news featured a successful San Antonio law firm in which all the partners were women. *They'll understand.* I called them the next day.

On November 14, 1994, in the comfortable offices of Dysart, Bennack, Malone and Specia, P.C., I told my story once more, this time to Cynthia F. Malone, attorney at law. As I had hoped, she did understand and agreed to take my case, and over the next month, she and her staff researched the army regulations applying to the commander's behavior. Two sections from the Army's court-martial manual seemed particularly relevant to my situation: Article 93, *Cruelty and maltreatment to a subordinate*, which includes the offenses of assault and sexual harassment, and Article 133m *Conduct unbecoming an officer and a gentleman*, which speaks to acts of "dishonesty, unfair dealing, indecency, indecorum, lawlessness, injustice, or cruelty."

On December 19, 1994, Cynthia Malone sent the following certified letter (return receipt requested) to Lt. Col. Smith stating:

CPT Linda Fischer has retained my services with regard to a claim of sexual assault and harassment by you from approximately December 1993 to July 1994. As her supervising officer, you misused your rank, position, and authority to subject CPT Fischer to actions which were cruel and oppressive in violation of Article 93 and 133 as cited above. Your actions, which are unbecoming to an officer, included unwanted sexual contact followed by continued sexual harassment creating an atmosphere of intimidation and hostility.

Your misconduct as her immediate supervisor demonstrates a lack of those moral attributes common to the ideal officer. This type of conduct and sexual harassment is in violation of Army Regulation 600-20 and punishable under Article 93 and 133 as cited above. As a result of your actions, CPT Fischer has received counseling to cope with the stress of the severe physical and mental abuse she experienced.

This letter is to request that you have no further contact with her, either verbally, physically, in writing, or through a third party. She further expects that you will not request that she serve in your command in the future. Should you attempt to contact CPT Fischer on this matter, she will not hesitate to file a formal complaint with the proper authorities. Your cooperation in this regard is appreciated.

Shortly before this letter was sent, I had asked Col. Mitchell, from Panama days, to meet me for lunch. Now that I was finally dealing with the events that occurred there, I wanted to clear up some issues.

"Did you ever tell Colonel Smith that I shouldn't receive my second command?" I asked pointblank, over a buffet lunch at the officers' club. Col. Mitchell raised his eyebrows quizzically and assured me he had not. I asked him several other questions about matters that hadn't added up for me in Panama, and his responses convinced me I could trust this man. Summoning my courage again, I told him about the assault. Although shock and alarm crossed his craggy face, he didn't dismiss my story.

"Why didn't you come to me, Linda?"

"I almost did once, sir," I replied, remembering the day I'd stood outside his office, agonizing about what to do.

"You should report this, you know," he advised.

Right...and see my career shot down in flames.

"I've sent a legal notice warning him to stop all direct or indirect contact," I told him, hoping he would leave it at that.

During the remainder of our lunch, the colonel didn't pressure me further. He did ask if I had told Jim, however. Although he'd never met my boyfriend, anyone who ever visited my office in Panama had heard me brag about the good-looking guy in all the pictures.

I lowered my eyes. "I haven't," I said. "But I can't think of anything better than being with him in Hawaii."

Shortly after Christmas, I learned that Lt. Col. Smith had signed for the attorney's letter on December 24. Surely now that he'd received the legal notice ordering him not to initiate contact with me, he would have the good sense to back off, and I would never hear from him again.

Unfortunately, right after the holidays Col. Mitchell called me with some disturbing news.

"I'm sorry to tell you that Colonel Smith called me and asked about you, Linda."

No! He won't go away? Not even after that letter? Instead he keeps invading my space and checking on me. Enough!

I decided to report the assault.

Navigating the Bureaucracy

That night, I hardly slept. Maybe that's not surprising considering the momentous decision I had made. It wasn't that I was having second thoughts. No, I knew I'd made the right decision, because the last year had almost destroyed me, taking me closer to a nervous breakdown than I could ever have believed possible. I didn't want to ever stand that close to the brink again, and I didn't want anyone else to, either. The truth must come out, so that *he* could never torment another subordinate. But knowing I'd made the right decision didn't erase the fear and anxiety I felt about what lay ahead. I'd heard too many stories of the little guy who reported the big guy and ended up getting the short end of the stick to believe that the process I was about to initiate would be easy.

The morning after Col. Mitchell called me, I drove through the Lackland AFB gates full of apprehension. My first order of business: talk to 1st Sgt. Perez. I owed this competent, dedicated soldier an explanation of what was about to transpire. He had undoubtedly already sensed something out of the ordinary, and I knew I would be placing and receiving some unusual phone calls from now on.

When I poked my head into 1st Sgt. Perez' office, I found him meeting with a couple of soldiers.

"Good morning, all," I said quietly. And then, to my first sergeant, "When you're done, I have a few things to talk to you about."

I walked down to my office. Sunlight streamed through the window, although the air conditioner kept the room cool. While waiting for the first sergeant, I signed a few documents in my inbox, but my attention soon wandered. My gaze rested on the wall plaques, the trophies on shelves—triumphs of the past—and on the pictures of family, special friends, and Jim, under the glass on my desk.

I began to cry. Although I had carefully surrounded myself with the good parts of my life, with the happy memories, even here feelings of pain and anger intruded. *He's taken so much from me. But I can't undo the past. All I can do is make sure he never causes anyone else this much pain.*

By the time 1ˢᵗ Sgt. Perez edged into my office, I had my emotions under control, but as I was to learn over the next few months, tears often lurked close to the surface.

"Ma'am, how are you?" He obviously sensed my turmoil.

"Fine," I replied, using the word that had been my standard lie for so long. "But I'm going to share some difficult information with you. Some things happened to me in Panama, and it's important that you know what will be going on with me for the next little while."

I took deep breaths to stave off the tears that sprang instantly to my eyes, for no female soldier ever wants to be labeled a "crying woman." Digging deep for control, I told 1ˢᵗ Sgt. Perez that I had been assaulted by my commander in Panama, a man I still feared. That was why I had asked to have my phone calls screened, I explained. The first sergeant listened carefully without interrupting, but I could see the caring in his eyes.

"I'm so sorry, ma'am," he said at last.

"I'm going to initiate an investigation by reporting this to the DAIG," I told him. During the night I had decided to report the assault to the Department of the Army's Inspector General in Washington D.C. because I wanted to avoid an investigation by CID (Criminal Investigation Division). CID is an arm of the military police, of which Lt. Col. Smith was a high-ranking officer, so it seemed to me the DAIG would be more likely to carry out an impartial investigation.

"Do you have the DAIG phone number, ma'am?" 1ˢᵗ Sgt. Perez asked.

When I replied in the affirmative, he said, "If you need anything, let me know."

I soon discovered I needed all my patience and persistence—and that of 1ˢᵗ Sgt. Perez as well—to navigate my way through the military bureaucracy. I expected that because I was an Army officer working on an Air Force installation, I might have some difficulty, but I couldn't have imagined the extent. I began by calling the Washington D.C. number.

"You have to talk to your local IG Office at Fort Sam Houston, ma'am."

So I did, and they referred me to another office.

"It's not our case because you're assigned to Lackland AFB, ma'am. You need to call Sergeant Williams at 721-7632."

Of course, Sgt. Williams referred me to another office, and so on. I called every EO (Equal Opportunity) and IG (Inspector General) office within a 50 mile radius plus the DAIG three or four times that day, spending over two hours on the phone with absolutely no success. In fact, I ended up exactly where I started—talking to the DAIG personnel in Washington, D.C.

Finally I stomped down to 1st Sgt. Perez' office. "You're not going to believe this, but I can't get anyone to take the case."

"You're kidding, ma'am."

"I wish I were. I've called all of these numbers at least twice and talked to every IG office in Texas, I think." I showed him the list of names and numbers—checked, crossed off, rechecked.

"Let me try, ma'am," he suggested.

"Sure thing," I said, passing him the list.

Much later, the sergeant was the one stomping down the hall. "Same thing, ma'am, and it's just not right! I say we call the CG's office." The CG was the Fifth Army commanding general stationed at Fort Sam Houston.

Finally, a suggestion that worked! I was able to speak directly with the Fifth Army Inspector General, and I made an appointment to meet with someone at their office the next day. You would think an EO or IG representative would say "I'm not certain who you need to talk to. Give me your name and number and I'll get back to you." Or, better yet, "Would you come to our office?" *Any EO or IG representative should realize that the victim may only muster the*

*courage to make one cry for help. As I had tried to do when
I stood outside Col. Mitchell's office that day in Panama.*

That night was another anxious one for me. I knew
I would have to tell my story again, and each time I did, I
relived the pain of those days. It felt like removing a ban-
dage from a wound that hadn't completely scabbed over.
With every telling, the scab was ripped away again. How
could the wound ever heal?

The next day I drove my little red convertible to
Fort Sam Houston, where two soldiers with the Inspector
General's office, a Maj. Sinclair and a Sgt. Humphrey,
questioned me for what seemed like hours before conclud-
ing, "This is a criminal case. CID will have to investigate."

*Not CID! Some of Smith's closest friends are CID.
I need someone outside the MP world to conduct an investigation and provide a finding.*

"Can't you please conduct the inquiry?" I pleaded,
unable to control my agitation.

"Well, we'll check with our D.C. headquarters,"
Maj. Sinclair said, wrinkling her thin nose. "But, Captain
Fischer, have you really thought about this? Don't you know
requesting an investigation could do more to hurt you than
help you? Are you sure you want to go ahead with this?"

Her questions confirmed my worst fears. Although
I'd known from the beginning that reporting the assault
could negatively affect my career, the people I had talked to
until now had surprised me with their support, and I had
begun to hope that perhaps the Army would believe me after
all. Maj. Sinclair's words dampened that hope, and I didn't
respond to her questions. *No turning back now, Linda.*

The sergeant changed the subject. "Have you
notified your chain of command?"

"Not on the Army side of the house," I replied. As
an Army officer working for the Air Force, I had little
contact with my official Army superior. However, because I
was connected to the Military Policy Academy, I decided to
inform the academy's commander, a General Clifton,
immediately. When I returned to my office, I told 1st Sgt.
Perez my plans.

"I'll place a call to Headquarters in the morning, ma'am, letting them know you need to speak to the commander under the open door policy," he said, ever efficient. The general's open door policy allowed any soldier in his command to see him personally. "I'll let you know the time as soon as it is coordinated. Now go home, ma'am, and get some rest."

My sergeant's last comment was his polite way of saying I looked a wreck, which wasn't surprising. I was totally exhausted from telling and retelling my story. Every night I lay down praying for sleep, then when the nightmare returned, as it almost always did, fighting to stay awake.

Many of my days seemed like nightmares, too. The morning after my visit to the IG office, I received a call from a Criminal Investigation Division officer, asking if I wanted to initiate an investigation. *What's going on? Who brought CID into this?*

"I'll call you when I'm ready to," I responded angrily.

When I called the IG office to complain that I hadn't wanted to involve CID, I was informed that "higher headquarters" had decided otherwise.

"At least you could have called me first," I said, "so I wouldn't be surprised." *The ball is rolling now. CID is taking over the investigation. It's out of my hands.*

Over the next several days I grew increasingly anxious because 1st Sgt. Perez had not been able to schedule a conference call with the general, and I feared that CID would get involved before my direct command had heard from me.

"I'm sorry, ma'am," 1st Sgt. Perez said. "This is much more difficult than it should be. I've called the commander's secretary and told her your request is personal. She wants you to call her."

When I called, the secretary asked, "Why do you want to talk to the commander, Captain Fischer?"

"It's personal," I said.

"Well, we have to know the topic."

"It's personal," I repeated.

"We'll have to call you back," and she hung up.

The next morning, the commander's aide called and took me through the routine again.

"Why do you need to talk to the commander?"

"I want to speak to him under the open door policy. The matter is personal in nature."

"We'll have to call you back."

By the time the deputy commander called me, I was pretty hot under the collar. *So much for the open door policy!*

"Captain Fischer, I understand you want to talk to the commander under the open door policy. What is the nature of the call?"

"It's personal, sir."

The deputy tried once more. "You know he will probably tell me whatever you tell him."

"That's his prerogative as commander, " I said. "But it was recommended that I speak directly to him."

He replied with the now famous closer, "I'll have to call you back."

1st Sgt. Perez was furious at the run-around I was receiving. "This is an outrage! The whole point of the open door policy is to avoid red tape! I'll bet none of these people has even spoken with the commander about this. Let me call Command Sergeant Major Escalante. He'll talk to the commander directly."

And he did. Before the day was over, I had an appointment for a conference call with the commander, General Clifton, at 0900 the next day—thanks to a couple of "get-it-done" noncommissioned officers!

Promptly at 9:00 the next morning, the general's secretary called. "This is the commander's office. Is Captain Fischer ready for the call?" Her voice was much friendlier today.

"Ma'am, I am on the line," I said.

When I recognized the general's voice, my heart raced. Although I'd met him once, I certainly didn't know him well or how he might react to the bearer of such news.

"Sir, this is Captain Fischer. I command the Training

Detachment here at Lackland Air Force Base. I am calling to inform you that I will initiate an investigation against my previous commander for sexual assault while serving as company commander in Panama. I'll be initiating the investigation through the CID office at Fort Sam Houston." I spoke as succinctly as I could.

The general was gracious. "Captain Fischer, thank you for your call. I understand that you had difficulty setting up this appointment under my open door policy, and I apologize for any inconvenience this may have caused you. I have talked to both my secretary and my aide to preclude this from happening in the future."

"Thank you, sir," I said.

"Further I would like to brief Colonel Turlow, my deputy, on this, with your permission," the general said. "He will keep me posted on the status of the case."

"Yes, sir. Thank you for your time, sir." And that was that.

Now that I had notified my chain of command, I felt free to call the Fort Sam Houston's CID office.

"Who will be serving as the investigator on my case?" I asked a chief warrant officer there. Since my conversation with Maj. Sinclair, I'd realized how important it would be to have an experienced investigator. I explained my concerns to the CID officer.

"We'll put our best agent on the case," he assured me. "Can you come in tomorrow?"

The next day found me sitting in my car outside the CID office. Directly across the street, I could see the MP company building where several soldiers from Panama now served, including Lt. Col. Smith's old driver, for one, and 1st Sgt. Lewis.

I don't want anyone to see me walking into CID. What if the system doesn't support me? But I know I'm doing the right thing. The system will support me. The Army will take care of me. By tomorrow my report will be in the military police blotter. Every MP at Fort Sam Houston will know my secret. Can I do this? I can do this. I must do this. I can't live with it any longer. And he mustn't do what he did to me to anyone else. The short walk from my car to the CID door was as long a walk as any I've ever taken.

I spent the next four hours inside a small, windowless room. Special Agent Cohen, a husky woman with a professional but easy-going manner, sat at a metal gray desk where she would record my answers on her computer. She broke the ice gently.

"Ma'am, I know this will be hard for you. I'll start off with getting some general information, but if at any time you feel uncomfortable or need a break, let me know, and I'll stop."

"Okay." I breathed deeply and sat as straight as I could in the uncomfortable chair. This was it.

Getting the general information out of the way didn't take long.

"What unit were you assigned to in Panama? When did you arrive in Panama? What was your rank? Who did you work for? What was his name? Where did he work? Was he married? What was her name?"

However, when Special Agent Cohen began to question me about specific events leading up to the assault, I couldn't control my tears.

"How long were you at the club? How many drinks did you have? When did you leave? Why did you leave with the commander? Why did you go into the house? What happened in the house? Where was his wife? Why did you go to the living room?"

I needed several breaks—to wipe my face or get some water—when the time came to describe the assault itself. Although by now I'd shared the *fact* of the assault with several people, this was the first time I'd had to go into detail. Feelings of shame and dirtiness almost overwhelmed me.

"What happened in the bedroom? When he held you down on the bed, was there penetration? What happened next? When did you leave?"

To make recounting my story even more difficult, I wasn't able to complete my statement in one sitting. I had certain responsibilities to my command and had to return to

Lackland for a planning meeting. Later I drove back to Fort Sam Houston where Special Agent Cohen continued her questions until late into the evening.

When she was wrapping up her questions, I had an idea that I thought might help her investigation. "I'd be willing to take a polygraph," I volunteered.

"Oh, no," she said. "That won't be necessary. We don't ask for lie detector tests in investigations like these. I think we have plenty of information from you."

By the time I left for home, my body ached as if I had the flu, and my eyes were swollen. But tired as I was, a restful night of sleep escaped me, for I knew I had to return to the CID offices in the morning.

The next day, after the CID chief reviewed my statement, I was asked to clarify some issues and to share names of soldiers who had served with me in Panama. Who might have noticed my commander's unusual behavior? I suggested a number of names: Colonel Mitchell; several majors: Davidson, Hansen, Middleton; first sergeants: Martinez, Lewis, and Price; Staff Sergeant Gordon, the female sergeant I'd gone to bat for; the Knights, and a number of my golfing buddies.

I knew interviewing these soldiers would take time. Although Col. Mitchell, 1st Sgt. Lewis, and several others were stationed here in the San Antonio area, most were scattered all over the country. The local CID would have to send out requests for assistance from other offices.

But at least the worst is over, I thought. Nothing could be more painful than reliving my experience in such detail. Little did I know!

Searching for a Falling Star

I knew the word was out when people from my past began to call, offering their sympathy. One of the first persons I heard from was the female soldier I had gone to bat for in Panama.

"Ma'am, Sergeant Gordon here. I just wanted to call and say I'm sorry to hear about the investigation. If you need anything, please call."

"Thanks," I said.

I felt comforted to know that at least some of the soldiers investigators would be talking to were supportive. So I felt doubly betrayed when I learned that immediately after Staff Sgt. Gordon was interviewed by the investigators, she called Col. Mitchell and asked, "Do you believe her, sir?" in a tone that implied *she* certainly didn't. Soon I heard of others who were encouraging me to my face, but questioning my integrity behind my back and spreading rumors, and I lost confidence in almost everyone except for Col. Mitchell.

That first month after the investigation began, January of 1995, was rough. Although the frequency of my nightmares had eased since I'd told my story, my days were full of uncertainty, and I felt the need to take control of other areas of my life. For example, I needed to work out some things in my relationship with Jim, who was still living in Hawaii. Although we'd spoken on the phone occasionally during the past year, I'd never told him about the assault.

I'd known I loved Jim for years, since the month we met in fact. At the time, spring of 1989, I was attending an officer training program at Fort Dix, New Jersey. When I wasn't working, I played racquetball at the post gym. One day, while playing on the challenge court with a burly soldier, I got off some great shots. It was one of those days when I could place the ball right where I wanted it and then return anything hit to me. Not until the fifth match did I lose to my opponent, and even then, not by much—15-14. The intensity of the games had collected quite an audience, and afterwards one of the guys who'd been watching said he knew someone I should play.

"Okay with me," I replied.

"Tomorrow at noon," the soldier said with a grin.

Right then I had a funny feeling I was being set up to play with one of the best. I was a pretty good player, able to give the average guy a run for his money, but great I was not. Maybe I need an edge, I thought. So that evening I bought a new shirt and a pair of spandex tights. The brightest tights you ever saw—pink and green and blue and orange neons that practically glowed in the dark. If you know how a new pair of athletic shoes makes you feel before the big race, you know how those shorts pumped me up. Wearing them, I could beat anybody. Or so I felt.

The next day I arrived at the courts early so I could get in a good warm-up. Then, right before noon, I headed out of the gym to get a breath of fresh air. I pushed my goggles up on my head and bounced the ball off the ground. Although a nippy March breeze blew, the sun shone brightly. I felt good.

At first I barely noticed the two soldiers walking toward me. But when the taller one said, "What's with the shorts?" I couldn't help but notice his engaging smile.

"These are my take-your-mind-off-the-game shorts," I said, laughing.

The two guys disappeared into the gym, while I bounced my ball outside for another few minutes before heading back inside for a long drink of water. I was warming up on the court by the time my noon opponent stepped on the court. Wouldn't you know it? He was the tall man with the great smile.

I could feel my cheeks flush. "Please excuse me," I said, stumbling over my words. "When I made that remark outside, I didn't know I would be playing you."

"No apology required," he said. "By the way, my name is Jim. And those shorts *do* look good."

"I'm Linda and I'm warmed up," I said. Which I

certainly was, because I think my blush could have heated the room. "The court is yours."

I tossed him the ball and leaned against the side wall. I'd found I could watch someone warm up and get a pretty good idea if there was any chance of winning, so I knew as soon as I saw those powerful arms slamming the ball against the wall that I was in trouble.

"Loser buys the winner a Pepsi," I said, not wanting the stakes to be too high. At least I could afford a can of pop.

Jim graciously gave me the first serve, instead of insisting on the traditional lob for it. Fortunately, I thanked him for his generosity then, because that first serve was all he gave me. From the very beginning, he clearly outmatched me, and the final score wasn't even close. No matter who you play, racquetball is always a fast-paced game. The ball screams by you, smashes off the ceiling, off the walls, and you have to stay alert all the time. With somebody like Jim, though, racquetball can be downright devastating. He was a master of the "kill shot"—a shot that you can't possibly return. But my competitive nature loves a challenge, and I never stopped trying.

Afterwards I waited in the hall for him to shower so that I could pay up with a Pepsi from a vending machine near the gym entrance. We took our sodas to the bleachers ringing the basketball court and chatted for awhile, and I learned that Jim was a sergeant stationed at Fort Dix, that he was the son of a Caucasian father and a Puerto Rican mother, and that he loved sports. He learned a little about me, and before we knew it, we'd decided to meet for dinner that night.

In the crowded, noisy restaurant, I grinned when my new friend Jim ordered a baked potato with his meal and blue cheese dressing for his salad. Something else we had in common. While he ate his steak, potato, and salad with blue cheese dressing, I ate my chicken, potato, and salad with blue cheese dressing and we talked and talked. This time I learned that he was a little older than me, that he'd grown up in Florida and California where he'd played football and other sports, and that he officiated at sports events after work hours. By now I knew I really liked this tall guy with the curly dark hair, so I was glad we arranged another get-together before we parted.

A few days later, we picked up some sandwiches and headed to a picnic area overlooking a small pond next to the post golf course. The weather was unusually nice for March in New Jersey, and the sun warmed our faces as we sat on wooden bleachers and talked. The more we were together, the more I regretted that I'd have to leave Fort Dix in a few weeks. The days passed too quickly, and by the time I returned to Fort Monmouth, I knew I was in love with Jim.

We managed to visit each other every couple of weeks—Fort Monmouth was about two hours from Fort Dix—and our relationship grew, but our visits were never long enough. Then came word that the Army was moving Jim to Hawaii in April. Remembering my early adolescent years in Hawaii, I envied Jim and wished I could have gone with him. But the Army had other plans for me, and I was committed to my career. Being apart from loved ones has always been the most difficult part of Army life for me.

That year Jim invited me to Hawaii for the Christmas and New Year's holidays. What a treat! Hawaii was more beautiful than I remembered, and our days together zipped by while we went to the beach, played golf and racquetball, and shopped for Christmas presents.

As soon as I arrived, I bought a miniature Christmas tree for his apartment and decorated it carefully. Then, during the days before Christmas, we placed our beautifully wrapped gifts to each other under the tree. We even bought stockings and stuffed them with cute little presents and treats. I'll never forget that first Christmas together—it's one of my happiest memories, ever.

Being in Hawaii gave me a chance to take a trip down memory lane with Jim as my guest. How I enjoyed introducing him to my favorite local spots. One beautiful sunny day, we were sitting in his apartment when I told him how my family had loved Haleiwa Beach on Oahu's North Shore.

"Let's go," he said.

So we packed up our beach gear and a lunch and off we went. But I'd forgotten how quickly weather can change in the Islands. The closer we got to Haleiwa, the darker the clouds grew. By the time we spread out our towels, the white sand beach was deserted. However, I was determined this would be a great day. Soon the clouds hung so low that we could no longer see the magnificent Waianae Range on our left. Then a cold rain began to pelt us until we were forced to huddle together under our towels, laughing at our predicament.

Before long, we headed back to Waikiki where the sun, in true Hawaiian style, almost always shines. On our way, we stopped for one of my favorites—a shave ice. Although "shaved" might sound more grammatical, if you want to be a local, you've got to ask for a "shave" ice, a heaping snow cone that is literally shaved off huge blocks of ice and then dribbled with your favorite syrup flavor. I chose orange; Jim chose cherry. Ah, this was the life!

Another day I talked Jim into a trip to another favorite childhood memory: the Toilet Bowl at Hanauma Bay. Hanauma is a protected fish refuge where tourists flock to snorkel among bright tropical fish, but locals like to head for the Toilet Bowl, a large hot-tub sized hole in lava rock that allows surf to surge in and out, tossing around those brave enough to venture in. As a kid, I would stand in the Toilet Bowl, waiting for the rush of water, and feel the same excitement mixed with fear that I felt on roller coasters.

When Jim and I arrived at Hanauma, I recalled that you had to walk on slippery, surf-wet ledges out to the far end of one of the half-moon bay's two sides. Unfortunately, only after we trekked all the way out one side, did I realize that my memory hadn't served me well. The Toilet Bowl was on the other side. Back we went, Jim game for anything. When we finally reached our destination, I was surprised to see that the lava hole was a lot smaller than I remembered. We watched kids jumping in and out for awhile and then returned to the beach where we laid out on towels and absorbed the sun's rays. Believe me, we were tired that night, not just from our play in the sun but also from hiking twice the distance we'd originally planned.

Perhaps my favorite memory of that trip is New Year's Eve, which we celebrated in a hotel ballroom, listening to Ray Charles. I dressed to kill—gold blouse, black leather skirt, high heels—and my hair piled in curls on the top of my head. Jim wore a suit, a very rare occasion in Hawaii. We sat at a table near the back of the ballroom and danced near our table whenever we felt like it. I savored each precious moment during this night of romance and music. He held me close when we danced, and we kissed on the stroke of midnight. How could the days have flown so quickly, I wondered?

Soon I was boarding a plane, my heart torn.
I already knew I would be leaving for Panama in April, and I was looking forward to duty outside the States, but when would I see Jim again? How I hated always having to say goodbye.

I didn't see Jim again for over eighteen months. Although we talked on the phone, I found that once I had my own command, I couldn't get away easily, so it was August, 1993, before I returned to the Islands. Now Jim was living on what we call the Windward side in a beautiful little place on the beach. Every morning we woke to the sounds of gentle waves meeting the sand. Jim would go to work and I would spend the day running and swimming before heading to Waikiki to meet him. In the evenings, we'd often enjoy dinner and a movie. If Jim was officiating a basketball game, I'd go sit in the bleachers and watch—not just the game but the handsome guy in the black and white shirt. Sometimes I volunteered to help with the clock or the score book when needed.

We stayed busy and I wished the days would never end. We each had a career, a world apart now, but inside, I believed we would someday be together. When this trip was over, there would be another.

Unfortunately, we drifted apart during the months after that trip. Jim was sent temporarily to the Sinai, and I was overwhelmed by my situation with the colonel. During my last months in Panama, I rarely talked to Jim. After the closeness we'd shared, how could I hear his voice and still keep my secret?

After I transferred to San Antonio, I thought perhaps we could resume our relationship, and I sent a note to Jim, letting him know where I was and how to contact me. He sent a note back telling me he was glad to be in contact again, so I called and thanked him for the note. How good it was to hear his voice and know that he still cared. For the next few months, thanks to the time difference between Texas and Hawaii, I mostly talked to his machine and he to mine, but when we did connect, I felt the magic again and wished we could be together.

One night I sat in my Texas apartment feeling particularly lonely and depressed. I'd been hearing more stories about so-called friends who now questioned my truthfulness, and I missed Jim terribly. He'd always been such a good friend as well as a lover. That night I wrote this song:

Searching for a Falling Star

*I look up in the night searching for a falling star
So I can make a wish to have you here beside me now
But my wish won't come true,
If you don't want me, too.*

*Seems like yesterday, since I last saw you,
When you hold me in your arms and whispered,*
*   "I love you."*
*How time and distance come between us
Still I love you, how I love you, and...*

*I look up in the night searching for a falling star
So I can make a wish to have you here beside me now
But my wish won't come true,
If you don't want me, too.*

Through the years, our love has blossomed.
With few yet precious moments, it has grown
In my thoughts and dreams. You're always with me.
Oh what joy, these sweet memories bring, so...

I look up in the night searching for a falling star
So I can make a wish to have you here beside me now
But my wish won't come true,
If you don't want me, too.

Here today I stand before you.
Take my hand, don't let it slip away.
Take my love, the passion that I offer,
Let us join, let us be as one.

I look up in the night searching for a falling star
So I can make a wish to be with you forever now.
But my wish won't come true,
If you don't want me, too.

After writing those words, I had to admit how much
I longed to visit Jim and Hawaii, but I knew the only way to
truly renew our relationship was to tell him about the last
year—the assault, its aftermath, my imposed silence, and the
situation surrounding the investigation.

I took a deep breath and dialed his number. When
his voice—not on an answering machine, but the real
thing—came through the lines, I told my story again. Thank
God his responses were warm and comforting, and for once
I didn't feel ashamed of my tears.

"Should I still come?" I asked near the end of our
conversation.

"Yes," he said without a second's hesitation. That
lack of hesitation combined with the warmth in his voice
eased my soul that night, and on February 20, 1995, I
boarded a plane to Hawaii. I'll never forget that trip.

Despite Jim's sympathetic reaction to my story, I
couldn't help but feel nervous about seeing him again, and I

hadn't slept well for several days. I settled myself in the narrow seat, patted a pillow into a comfortable shape behind my head, and closed my eyes, hoping that I could get some rest on the long flight to Hawaii.

The next thing I know I'm in a hotel room—one where Jim and I are staying together. I'm dressing for dinner in my prettiest dress, because Jim and I are going to a nice restaurant and I want to look my best for him. He stands at the door of our room, looking sharp in a dark suit, telling me that he is going downstairs to check something out and that I should meet him in a waiting room near the lobby. Then he's gone and I'm brushing my hair once more and smoothing on lipstick. Ready at last. I grab my purse and head for the elevator with a little bounce in my step, smiling at the thought of the evening ahead. I step into the elevator and hit the button for the lobby. What a wonderful evening this will be!

When the elevator doors open, I step out into the lobby. A figure comes towards me. I don't pay much attention until, as I head for the waiting room where I will meet Jim, the figure moves to cut me off. I see the figure's face— Lt. Col. Smith's face. I stop abruptly, an icy feeling overwhelming me. A strange paralysis grips my limbs and my lips. I can't move or talk. The commander's lips are moving, however, speaking words I can't hear at first. I look around frantically, searching for help, and then his muttering voice becomes clear. "I just want to talk to you, I have to know how you feel."

Somehow those words release me from paralysis, and I begin to run. But I can't find the waiting room or Jim. While I run, I can sense the commander waiting patiently, as if he knows there is no escape for me. I run on through hotel halls. I don't know where I am. I must have gotten turned around. What will I do?

When my body jerked in terror, I awoke to the humming of the plane engine. Another nightmare! Not an entirely new one, but one that includes Jim and increases my anxiety about seeing him again. How will the assault affect my ability to be intimate with him? Will I be able to truly give myself to one man if another haunts my nights? I did not sleep again on that flight.

Butterflies danced in my stomach when the plane finally touched down at the Honolulu airport and when I walked up the long ramp exiting the plane. But then I saw Jim, his face split with that wonderful smile, I heard the warmth and tenderness in his voice, and it was as if we had never been apart.

Since my last trip, Jim had finished his twenty-plus years of Army service and now ran a small business in Waikiki where he also lived. We put my luggage away in his apartment and went for a walk on Kalakaua Avenue, a main street lively with tourists. But I was exhausted from the trip, so our walk was brief, and soon we headed back to his place.

That night was like a spiritual awakening as I discovered that although the commander had ripped my life apart, he had not destroyed my soul. In Jim's arms, I found love and peace and the knowledge that I *could* give myself and my love to the right man. Blessedly, no thoughts of that horrible night in Panama intruded to mar my happiness.

For the rest of my visit, Jim and I ran and enjoyed the sun and the scenery, but we spent much time talking seriously, too. We decided to go forward and work on our relationship, although we both knew it would remain a long-distance one for the time being. Leaving Jim was even more difficult this time, but I returned to Texas refreshed and invigorated, ready to face my uncertain future in the Army. And with at least one thing to look forward to—a visit from Jim in September.

Mind Games

Less than a week after I returned to San Antonio, Special Agent Cohen called me from her Fort Sam Houston office with a surprising request.

"Captain Fischer, we would like you to see a psychiatrist at Fort Hood."

A psychiatrist? Why would CID ask me to see a psychiatrist when they had refused my offer to take a polygraph?

"Why?" I asked.

Special Agent Cohen hesitated briefly. "Because they want to see if you are making this up or...or perhaps hallucinating."

Her words struck me like a physical blow. *Does the Army think I'm crazy?* But on reflection, I realized a military mind might look at it that way. No one in her right mind would report an incident like this, so I *must* be crazy for coming forward. I asked Special Agent Cohen a few questions about what to expect, but in the end I agreed. After all, I had nothing to hide.

One bright sunny morning in March, I set out from San Antonio for an afternoon appointment in Fort Hood, a four-hour drive away. The closer I got to Fort Hood, the more uneasy I grew. I knew I wasn't hallucinating, but I'd never seen a psychiatrist, and it's hard not to get paranoid when you go up against power. From my frequent calls to Special Agent Cohen, I knew that Lt. Col. Smith hadn't even made a statement, other than to insist on a lawyer. And he had refused to take a polygraph, which came as no surprise to me. No way would he pass! So he surely wouldn't agree to a psychiatric examination either. I was willing to submit to all sorts of indignities to help the Army learn the truth; he wasn't. Despite his lack of cooperation to date, he was both male and a higher ranking officer than I—two qualifications that I was painfully learning counted a lot in the Army.

When I drove through Fort Hood's gates, I had no problem finding my way around, because I'd been stationed here back in 1983 when I first enlisted in the Army. The good old days, I reflected. That first year I was a Specialist Fourth Class and lived on base, but was able to visit my family every weekend. What good times we had!

My sister's marriage had recently ended, and she and her two little girls, Mahialani and Luzinda, had settled in Georgetown where Anna found a job at the university. As I watched her start a new life as a single parent, I admired her strength and courage. At the time, I drove a used Malibu—not a fancy car, but good enough to get me around—and it gave me real pleasure to give Anna that car and pay the insurance until she got on her feet.

Once she had the Malibu, she and her little girls would come to Ft. Hood every Friday to pick me up and take me to Mom and Dad's where we would relax until Sunday afternoon, when Anna would drive me back to Fort Hood. In the summer we pitched washers in the backyard; in the winter we watched football, the "Boys," of course. But always I enjoyed the knowledge that I was finished with high school and college and able to spend time with my family.

During the week, I lived in the barracks a few blocks away from the hospital. I worked as a personnel actions clerk, processing administrative paperwork, a job I knew I was good at. And I participated in all the sports I could—softball and racquetball—and of course I always enjoyed running.

I also volunteered to be a member of the Opposing Forces for field exercises occasionally. The Opposing Forces are the bad guys, the enemy, the troops that attack the good guys. We used sniper fire, night attacks, ambushes—whatever we could—to help the good guys prepare to face the real thing someday.

All in all, life was good, and I soon considered myself your basic gung-ho soldier. I didn't take any flack: especially from guys. I remember one particular group of soldiers who would sometimes walk behind me when I went to lunch at the cafeteria. It was just coincidence; they were going to lunch at the same time. Whenever they saw me, they would start in with their macho comments and catcalls.

"Oh, isn't she cute?"

"Bet I could make you happy."

"Wanna go out with me?"

One day I had had enough. I spun around to face them, bringing them up short right in front of me. Then I read them the riot act.

"You're acting like jerks! How would you like it if guys walked behind your moms or your sisters saying the things you say?"

Guilty looks spread across their faces, and several of them apologized. One, braver than the rest, asked if I would have lunch with them.

"No," I said. "I need to see if you can behave yourselves. When you've proved you can conduct yourselves like gentlemen, I would consider having lunch with you."

"Yeah, yeah," they murmured to each other. Then to me, "That's what you say now." Obviously they didn't believe I'd ever eat lunch with them, much less speak to them again.

They did get the message about their inappropriate behavior, however, and for the next few weeks, I walked to lunch undisturbed. Then one morning they showed up in my office.

"Now will you come to lunch?" said the brave one.

"Sure," I said. I could tell my acceptance surprised them, but off we went to the first of several lunches together, and those soldiers never bothered me with disrespectful behavior again.

So I had much to be thankful for during those days—a comfortable job, plenty of friends, my family close by—but after a year, I found myself ready to move on to something more challenging. A promotion to sergeant, I supposed. My section supervisor, Sgt. Thomas, had other ideas.

"You should apply for Officer Candidate School," he said.

Naturally my father agreed and pressed me to start the necessary paperwork. By this time, I knew the Army was a comfortable fit for me, so in September,1983, I initiated my application to OCS. The process was a lengthy one— with physicals, boards, and the ever-present paperwork—but in March of 1984, I heard I'd been accepted. I'd earned a chance to serve my country as an officer! I could hardly wait to tell my parents, for I knew my career military father would be thrilled. He was, of course, and my whole family celebrated at my next three-day pass.

Today, passing through the doors of the Ft. Hood hospital, I remembered that celebration. It seemed so long ago. Then I was on a high, looking forward to what I never doubted would be a successful career in the military. Now I was feeling pretty low, exhausted from sleepless nights and anxiety-filled days. Although I'd earned my promotion to major, I could hardly celebrate the way my career was going. Not when I was pushing a buzzer that would allow me entrance to a mental ward.

What am I doing here? Do they think I'm some kind of nut? Why are they checking me out? Why can't they realize he's the sick puppy! I walked past the nurses' station toward the psychiatrist's office, past patients wearing hospital gowns and goofy slippers on their feet. *Does the Army think I belong on a ward like this?* Taking a deep breath, I tried to prepare myself, knowing that just telling my story would take much out of me, emotionally and physically.

A lanky, sharp-featured doctor greeted me at the door of his office in Ward Five West. Although I did not know it then and never would have guessed it from his small, bare office, Lt. Col. Staley was a graduate of one prestigious university and a professor at another. He invited me to take a seat.

I was nervous at the start of our interview, but Dr. Staley soon put me at ease. He began with a few basic questions of who I was and where I worked, then asked me about my childhood. By the time he asked about the events in Panama, I felt somewhat reassured. Although I couldn't tell for sure whether or not he believed me, at least I was being treated with respect.

The interview took two hours. When Dr. Staley rose to say goodbye, he told me he would be sending a copy of his findings to the CID office and faxing a courtesy copy to me. I headed toward the nurses' station again, limp with exhaustion but feeling hopeful as well. The doctor had *seemed* to believe me, I thought. But I cautioned myself not to get my hopes too high. A nurse buzzed me out of the mental ward.

A few days later, my home fax spit out the doctor's report, and I read it avidly. It started right out by stating that the purpose of the examination was to evaluate my "credibility vis a vis all allegations" against Lt. Col. Smith. I wished again that some doctor would evaluate his credibility, but of course, he'd have to make a statement first. I read on, and as I did, I breathed a sigh of relief. While I didn't understand all the language I was reading, I did understand, "no evidence of hallucinations, delusions (persecutory or otherwise)." I learned that my sleeping problems, including "intrusive, vivid dreams," were a normal reaction to trauma, and that I showed no evidence of "Schneiderian symptoms." I didn't have any idea what Schneiderian symptoms were (and I still don't) but I knew not having them had to be good.

Near the report's end, I read: "Captain Fischer does not currently suffer from any DSM-IV psychiatric or disorder...based on her sincere presentation, the consistency of her story, the lack of any identifiable secondary gain, and predicated on the congruence of her post-assault psychological symptomology and the subsequent 'triggering' of her need to come to resolution engendered by her commander's congratulatory note, (CPT Fischer) is credible and in the professional opinion of the undersigned, a completely truthful witness/victim of the events she describes."

And then, words that I read over and over: "Further, in the opinion of the undersigned, the events as described by CPT Fischer support an opinion that LTC Smith used his 'authority relationship' to psychologically coerce CPT

Fischer to submit to not only the sexual advance, but also numerous episodes of racquetball, fishing, and other activities he insisted she engage in…In the professional opinion of the undersigned she is being completely truthful in her allegations."

At least one Army professional believed me! For several days, that fact buoyed my spirits. But that was about all the good news I received during the spring of 1995. Every other week or so, I would call Special Agent Cohen to ask how the investigation was going. About all I ever heard from her was that the process for interviewing soldiers from my past was taking a long time. Until one day in June when she called me.

"CID is requesting that you submit to hypnotism," she said.

Hypnotism? After I'd been subjected to a psychiatric evaluation? After I'd volunteered to take a polygraph test and been refused? I didn't know much about hypnotism, but I didn't like what I'd heard. Still, I'd "passed" the psychiatric examination, I knew I'd pass a polygraph, and I certainly wanted the Army to accept the truth, whatever that took. So I agreed, and we set a hypnotism session date in two weeks.

However, I knew I needed to learn more about hypnotism, so I began asking Special Agent Cohen lots of questions. What was the process actually like? Who would be there to ensure that the examiner only asked questions about Panama and the incident? Would I be able to review the questions they would ask me?

"That will all be explained to you," Special Agent Cohen would say.

Then, the day before my appointment, she called me at the office and dropped a bombshell. "There's been a change, ma'am. Your appointment has been canceled."

Canceled? I hadn't wanted to submit to hypnotism in the first place, but I had agreed and had spent much time and energy trying to prepare myself for the ordeal.

"How can you play around with people like this!" I yelled.

"Ma'am, we're only following orders from our

higher headquarters," she replied apologetically. I slammed
down the phone. I wasn't really angry at Special Agent
Cohen. How could I be when I knew the Army well enough
to realize that she had no choice but to follow orders? But I
was furious at the elusive "higher headquarters." Being
yanked around like this was agony. Especially when I knew
full well that the officer who harassed and assaulted me was
not experiencing the same kind of treatment.

During those spring months, my twice-monthly
counseling sessions with Chaplain Bennett were a real
comfort to me. In his office, I talked out some of my frustra-
tions and turmoil, and I'll always be grateful that he helped
me keep my feet on the ground during a difficult time.
Although I had gone to Protestant churches most of my life,
I began to attend his Catholic church, where I found a warm
welcome from his parishioners, especially from a young
couple about my age. Randy was an Air Force officer, Sarah
a school teacher, and we became close friends. If I didn't go
home on the weekend, I would often go to the movies and
dinner with Randy, Sarah, and Tim Bennett. I also continued
to officiate at intermediate school basketball games and
men's recreation league softball almost every weekday
evening. Chaplain Bennett's counseling, officiating and
being with friends or family kept me from becoming completely fixated on the investigation.

Another diversion about this time was a visit from
Millie, my Panama running buddy, who was now stationed
in Georgia. She had put together a team of women who
would be competing in the Army Marathon sponsored by
Fort Sam Houston, and she needed a place for her team to
stay. How about my apartment? Of course I couldn't refuse,
and six of us plus myself were soon packed into my place.

I hadn't run much for over a year or participated in
sports; the associations were too painful. This was a great
loss for me, because I'd been an avid sportswoman and
athlete since junior high. When Millie invited me out on
training runs with her team, I hesitated at first. I knew I was
out of shape, but to my surprise I had a great time. I volunteered to be part of the team's support crew for the race and

was thrilled to see them win. How wonderful to feel once again the excitement of being part of a winning team!

I hated to see Millie and her team leave, but I'm grateful that their visit helped me reclaim a precious part of my life. Running with them broke the barrier that had kept me from the kind of physical activity I had been used to. Now I could return to running and remember my times with the team, not those with the commander.

Then the possibility of being transferred to Hawaii resurfaced, bringing me new hope. I applied, and much to my surprise and joy, was informed that my transfer had been approved. Jim could cancel his September trip to Texas because I would be in Hawaii by August! To this day I am grateful to Col. Mitchell, who I believe had a hand in smoothing the way for me.

By this time Special Agent Cohen had told me my role in the investigation was complete. Now the ball was completely in CID's court, and all I could do was wait. So I busied myself those last few weeks before the move with packing, saying my good-byes, and driving to Moline, Illinois for Randy and Sarah's wedding. When I returned from Illinois, I found a note on my desk: Call CID.

"What's up?" I asked Special Agent Cohen.

"We have received a request that you take a polygraph," she said.

I didn't throw my phone across the room as I was tempted to do, but I did protest bitterly. "You told me everything was done. And you didn't think I should take a polygraph when I volunteered."

For the first time, I didn't agree on the spot to a CID request. Instead I asked, "Who's supposed to advise *me*? I'm the one getting pushed around, and the criminal is the one with the attorney."

That's when I learned that I could have been, *should* have been, talking with a Victim Liaison Representative right from the beginning. The Army had recently established a special office to assist victims, but both CID and the Inspector General's office had neglected to tell me about it. Now, as the investigation closed, I learned that a Victim

Liaison Representative was housed just blocks from Special Agent Cohen. Once more, the Army system had failed me.

Over the next few weeks, I met several times with Vivian Hightower, the civilian Victim Liaison Representative. She listened carefully to my story and to my confusion about whether or not I should take a polygraph.

Her advice was clear. "I don't recommend it," she said. "We never advise the victim to take a polygraph. Especially when the accused refuses to. Polygraphs can be difficult, because most of the time, victims of assault and rape tend to blame themselves in some way."

Still, I agonized over the decision. At one point, I called Col. Turlow, Deputy Commander for the Military Police School. The general had assigned him to be helpful to me back in January after I first reported the assault. At the time, the Deputy Commander had said, "We're here to support you. If you need any assistance, give me a call." And he had repeated his assurances when I'd visited the Military Police School back in May.

But now, after I explained my frustration about the investigation process and the recent polygraph request, there was a long silence from his end of the phone.

"I'm sorry. I can't help you," he said finally. "I know Lieutenant Colonel Smith personally."

I could not believe it. *And you didn't know Lt. Col. Smith personally a few months ago when you offered your assistance?* At that moment I felt terribly alone, again betrayed. This time by this officer. And, once again by the entire system.

Finally, taking Vivian Hightower's advice, I called Special Agent Cohen and told her I wouldn't submit to a polygraph.

"Then our investigation is complete," she said. "We will soon be forwarding all our information to Washington D.C., for further action."

Several days later, I boarded the plane for Hawaii with mixed emotions. On the one hand, I was happy to be on the way to my favorite islands, to Jim, to a new job. On the other, I felt pretty beaten down, and I knew my ordeal was not over by a long shot. Given the results of the psychiatric evaluation and the CID report, I believed that Lt. Col. Smith would face a court-martial which meant I would have to fly to Washington D.C. and testify. Not a pleasant prospect. After the experiences of the past six months, I dreaded the possibility of facing more betrayal and maltreatment. But I knew that all I could do now was move forward.

No Right To Know

Night had fallen when I arrived in Hawaii on August 14, 1995. My sponsor, Maj. Bierman, greeted me at the airport and drove me to the Hale Koa, the military hotel where I would be staying temporarily. As we drove toward Waikiki, I recognized a few of the buildings lighting up the skyline, and my anticipation for my new assignment grew. It felt like a new beginning. Obviously I had more to face—the ugliness of a court martial probably—but for now I was in a place I loved. I would see Jim tomorrow, and I assumed I'd have at least a couple of weeks to settle into my job and find a place to live before having to deal with the outcome of my case.

At the hotel, Maj. Bierman handed me a schedule that outlined the inprocessing to my unit that would begin the next day.

"I'll be by to pick you up at 7:00 a.m.," he promised. It was late, and I needed to get my uniform ready for tomorrow.

The next morning he was right on time, and I soon found myself reporting for duty at Fort Shafter, a small Army base west of downtown Honolulu. I would be working for the Engineers, providing security and law enforcement for an Engineer Division in a one-of-a-kind position. Maj. Bierman took me to my third story office, a good-sized room with an expansive view of the ocean, the city, and even Diamond Head. I placed my briefcase on the chair and took a deep breath. In a few minutes I would meet my co-workers, and although for most of my life, I'd felt quickly comfortable with new faces, my experiences of the past two years had changed me. Now I could never be sure what I was walking into.

Fortunately my new co-workers welcomed me warmly and soon I was able to put faces with voices I had talked to over the phone, including that of my new commander, Col. Wilcott, a deeply-tanned man with a shock of white hair. He gave me a friendly hello and handshake, but had only just explained that I would be meeting with him again in a few days when his secretary Samantha reminded him of another meeting.

As soon as he left the room, Samantha handed me a message. "Ms. Hightower, the Victim Liaison Representative from Fort Sam Houston, would like for you to give her a call," she said.

Vivian Hightower? Calling me so soon? I hoped my face hid my feelings, that Samantha couldn't tell my insides were churning. Surely the commander's secretary was wondering why a Victim Liaison Representative wanted to talk to Capt. Fischer. Glancing down at the note on the usual yellow form, I couldn't repress a touch of anger that the Panama nightmare was intruding when I hadn't even been on my new job for two hours. Maj. Bierman was continuing with office introductions, but flustered by the note, I hardly heard the names of the rest of my co-workers.

Finally, introductions concluded, Maj. Bierman noted that our next appointment would be at 10:00 a.m. and he would be back to collect me then. After he strode off down the hall, I returned to my office and sank into my new chair, trying to collect myself. I had not expected to face reminders of the investigation on my first day in Hawaii, and I could feel my hands begin to sweat and my heart speed up. I pushed myself out of my chair and headed out to Samantha's desk.

"How do I place this call to Texas?" I asked, as quietly as I could.

Without the slightest bit of curiosity in her cheerful voice, Samantha showed me which numbers to press for an outside line and which lines I could use.

"Don't forget the time difference," she reminded me.

Texas time was five hours ahead of Hawaii's, but it would still be working hours at Fort Sam Houston. Unfortunately, Ms. Hightower was away from her desk, so I had to leave a message in her voice mail box. No sooner had I hung up than Maj. Bierman was back. Talking to Ms. Hightower would have to wait until tomorrow; today I needed to concentrate on appointments, phone calls and paperwork.

After work, I was taken back to my hotel, and I drank in the blue sky and warm sun during the drive. The Hale Koa is an elegant military hotel facing the white sands of Waikiki, so the moment I closed the door of my room, I tore off my uniform, dressed in shorts, and headed outside. Walking along the beach brought me real joy because I knew this time I wouldn't have to leave Hawaii again in two weeks.

And then I was with Jim, who lived only a few blocks away. Happiness bubbled inside me. Just hearing his voice calmed me, and I felt safe with him, as if nothing in the world could harm me. We strolled along Kalakaua Avenue—the main drag—watching the sun set over the ocean, the horizon filling with an array of colors— pink and peach and violet—until the sky darkened into night and the stars came out. In the warmth of Jim's arms, I found comfort and peace. How wonderful it was to know that we would be able to spend more time together.

The next morning Maj. Bierman picked me up for work again, as he would until my car arrived from the mainland. Before the rush of appointments began, I called Vivian Hightower in Texas, and this time I reached her. She told me that the case had been closed.

"The prosecutor's office in D.C. has been trying to reach you. If you call Major Scott, he'll give you the disposition of the case," she said, giving me a number to call.

This shocked me. No one in D.C. had even contacted me. How could they have made a decision without talking to me?

My heart pounded and my stomach lurched uneasily as I dialed the number, but to my dismay, I was unable to reach Maj. Scott that day or for several days thereafter. A series of difficulties seemed to conspire against me. His office was moving from one location to another, the phone number was changing, and the time difference—six hours between Hawaii and the East Coast—didn't help. Finally, however, he and I connected.

"What is the disposition of the case?" I asked, after I

explained who I was.

"I'm not able to tell you," he replied.

"I beg your pardon?" I thought perhaps I'd misheard him.

"You don't have the right to know," he explained.

"I don't have the right to know how my own case was decided?" I protested bitterly. "Then why would you even bother to call me?"

"We are required to tell you that the case has been closed."

My confusion turned to rage. *I'll bet this means nothing has been done. He's gotten away with it! How can that be? But no matter what has happened, at least they should tell me the truth!* The insensitivity of the system and the investigation felt like a slap in the face, adding insult to injury.

"This is a sick joke," I blurted, unable to keep my cool any longer.

"No, ma'am," the major said. "We can't tell you the disposition of the case. You can, however, request the outcome of the case under the Freedom of Information Act from the CID Records Holdings Office."

"Well, that's just wonderful!" I snapped. "Thanks for nothing, sir!"

Tears rolled down my cheeks and my hand shook as I hung up the phone. Anger and pain whirled inside. I hurried to the restroom. *Nothing was done. Nothing! Nothing! How can that be?* I splashed cool water on my face and took deep breaths to regain my composure. In moments my life changed again. Although I felt as if the life had been sucked out of me, I had a full day ahead of me, and I was a professional. I'm not sure how I got through the day when all I really wanted was to be alone. I do know, however, that I was a different person when Major Bierman drove me home that evening. The bubbling excitement I had originally felt over being back in Hawaii had evaporated.

When I let myself dejectedly into my hotel room, I expected to spend a lonely evening because Jim was working. But the blinking message light on my phone brought welcome news. Chaplain Tim Bennett was in Hawaii, on his way to a new assignment in Korea. He'd told me he would call when he came through, and now here he was—for a week. His timing could not have been better.

We met for dinner at a Thai restaurant in Waikiki where I filled him in on the latest developments.

"It's upsetting that they won't tell me the case disposition when I was the victim," I explained. "I feel like they're hiding something."

"I can understand how frustrating it must be," he said. "And I admire your courage in fighting against what you feel is unjust."

Tim's empathetic responses always encouraged me, and before the evening was over, we had planned a trip to the beach and a luau for later in the week. Back in my room, I gave Jim a call. "Hello, this is Jim's personal secretary service, please leave your message, thank you." I loved to listen to the sound of his voice. I left a short message and I was off to sleep. Unfortunately, however, Jim's voice couldn't drive the nightmares from my sleep, and once again I spent a restless night with the demons of Panama.

All that week I worked hard, knowing that I would see Tim over the weekend. On Saturday, we headed for Hanauma Bay. This time I knew exactly how to get to the Toilet Bowl. Tim and I slipped into the lava hole letting the surge lift us high in the air, then holding our ground when it left so we wouldn't be sucked out to sea. Back in town that night, we ate dinner at Duke's, a great beach hangout where I was in love with the mango sauce ribs.

"How are you doing, Linda? Really?" Tim asked, watching my face closely. He must have seen the tiredness in my eyes.

"The dream has been coming back a lot," I admitted. "I fight sleep like a little kid who doesn't want to take a nap, tossing and turning until sheer exhaustion wins."

"You're a strong woman," he said encouragingly. "In time this will pass."

I hoped he was right, even though most of the time I couldn't see the light at the end of the tunnel. Still, I was

grateful for a day of fun and adventure and even more
grateful that I still had Monday to look forward to, when
Tim and I would meet again for a luau. On Sunday I went
for a run along the beach, and Hawaii worked its magic on
me once again. Under the warm sun, I could believe that a
power greater than me was watching over me.

Monday was a day of information overload as I
hustled around to appointments and stuffed my brain with
the details of my new job, and I was happy to learn that my
little red convertible had arrived and was ready for pickup.
Although Maj. Bierman had been more than helpful, now I
wouldn't have to rely on him for transportation. I could
begin to apartment hunt or just go for drives in the sun with
the top down. All in all, I was feeling more cheerful when I
met Tim for the luau.

"You can't go to a luau without a lei," I said, placing
a ring of fragrant, pale yellow plumeria around his neck and
kissing him on both cheeks in the traditional Hawaiian
greeting.

What fun we had that evening. Tim was picked to
dance on the stage, but he couldn't get those hips to swivel
nearly as well as the lovely hula dancers surrounding him.
His attempts led to much hilarity, however, and I grinned
when I snapped the pictures that would no doubt embarrass
him later. It was hard to say goodbye to him that evening,
for I knew it would be some time before I saw him again,
but his visit had cheered me immensely. He believed in me,
that I would survive these hard times, and that helped a lot.
I waved goodbye to him and then started into the lobby of
my hotel.

As always, the lobby was full of people, primarily
military personnel coming and going across the Pacific.
Suddenly I heard familiar voices; I saw faces I recognized.
Two officers I'd known from Panama days and their families stood no more than 20 yards from me. Stopping dead in
my tracks, I looked for a way to escape. I didn't want to talk
to Military Police officers. "Of the troops...for the troops,"
the Military Police Corps motto echoed in my head.
I turned, but not quickly enough.

"Linda?" one of the officers called.

My body shivered as I greeted the party with a forced smile, shaking hands and making polite small talk, explaining that I had just recently moved to the Islands. The officers told me that they were now stationed here, too, and I could tell from their eyes that they knew what had happened.

"I have to go," I said, as soon as I decently could. I moved toward the elevator, my heart pounding. I remembered what Col. Mitchell had said to me in San Antonio. *I'm sorry to have to tell you this, Linda. You can trust no one. They are not your friends.* Once again I felt the betrayal, the loss of camaraderie, that I'd hoped to put behind me when I moved to Hawaii. Once more the scabs were ripped from my wounds.

I think these guys know even more than I do. The Army won't tell me what happened, but these guys have the inside connection. They know nothing has been done, so they probably think I'm a liar. How can I ever work in the Military Police Corps again?

That night I thanked God that I was with the Corps of Engineers here in Hawaii. But I realized with great pain that reminders of shame and humiliation could follow me no matter where I went, no matter how many miles I put between me and Panama.

Settling in Paradise

Despite the bad moments during my first month in Hawaii, being with Jim again was wonderful. He had to spend long hours at his business and I had to apartment-hunt many evenings, but we managed to snatch precious time together. We often walked the beaches and streets of Waikiki, and soon I began to think I would have to add miles to my daily run just to work off the effects of the ice cream cones that became a routine treat during our walks.

I loved to watch the spark in Jim's eyes when he smiled and laughed. Moments with him brought relief to the emotional turmoil within me, as I struggled with the anger and pain that often threatened to overwhelm me. Sometimes I wished I could just go away with him. When he was beside me at night, the dreams didn't haunt me; without him, my sleep was restless and broken. Although I occasionally talked to Jim about my struggles with the Army bureaucracy, I didn't tell him about my nightmares. I valued his perspective and trusted his judgment, but I didn't want him to feel that he had to be the answer to my problems.

When my car arrived, I began my apartment hunt and soon I found just what I was looking for right in the heart of Waikiki— a two bedroom, one bath place twenty floors above the street with a great view of Diamond Head, the mountains, and the Pacific Ocean. From my kitchen window, I can see the great Pacific Ocean, and every morning before I leave for work, I look out this window at the waves, surfers, and boats in the deep blue water. In the evening,
I watch the sun set in a riot of colors over this same water. The lanai looks out over the Ala Wai Canal, a narrow strip of water from which the voices of paddlers practicing in their canoes waft up to me. The lanai also faces the steep, green mountains of Oahu, as does my master bedroom window. I love to gaze at these mountains, overhung by a changing sky that is usually blue but sometimes misty or bisected by

colorful rainbows.

When I first moved in, the apartment needed some fix-up, but I plunged in enthusiastically, since I didn't want to sleep. After work in the evenings, I removed old wallpaper and repainted the entire place. Then, once the new carpet was installed, I was ready for my household goods which had been in storage. A sleeping bag on the floor gets old after awhile!

Meanwhile I was working my way through file cabinets and desk drawers of paperwork at the office, getting a handle on what was what and where to find it. I had completed the staff briefings, but was still feeling my way around when I learned that I would be traveling extensively before Christmas—to Washington D.C., first and then to Korea, Japan, and Okinawa. I hoped to get the apartment in order before I left, so I spent my evenings unpacking boxes, arranging furniture and hanging pictures. Jim lived within walking distance in a Waikiki studio apartment, and I was anxious for him to see my place, but not until it was done. I wanted to make a good impression, because he hadn't been to a place of mine since we were in New Jersey six years earlier. I'd have him over for a special dinner before I left, I decided.

Gradually the pile of boxes in my apartment grew smaller until all that was left were my photo albums and the personal belongings I planned to take to my office. Over the years I'd kept two sets of fat photo albums, one set for family and personal photos, the other for pictures from work, and until that last year in Panama, I'd always kept them up to date. For the past two years, however, I'd let the task slide. So many of the snaps included Lt. Col. Smith. I knew eventually I'd have to deal with them, but I wasn't ready yet. For now I would store the boxes of photo albums and the packets of loose snaps in the spare room closet.

I set the boxes marked "office" by the front door so I could take them to work in the morning. I knew that I wouldn't find any surprises when I unpacked them, because they held only personal belongings I'd put up in my San Antonio office. No pictures of Lt. Col. Smith, just mementos soldiers had given me over the years. I missed those soldiers, missed having a command, but I was glad to have the plaques, pictures, and guidons that reminded me of them.

Although I worked hard at my job and at fixing up the apartment, I usually found time to exercise, too, encouraged by the ever-present island sun. Ever since Millie and the girls had visited me in San Antonio, I'd enjoyed running again, and I'd mapped out a few favorite running routes in Waikiki. In addition, I had my choice of swimming in the apartment building pool or at the beach just two blocks away, and the area offered great bike routes, too. I was in exercise heaven.

But I could not, *would* not, let the investigation die. The thought of Lt. Col. Smith still being in the Army despite his actions—and the threat this might pose to me and my career—gnawed away at me. As did the Army's recent treatment of me. Why couldn't they tell me the outcome of the investigation? The average non-military person would say, "A person who brings a charge is entitled to know the outcome." That was a given in our country's justice system. Why not in the Army? But not only was I refused information about the outcome of my case, the Army was also making it hard for me to get that information. For my own survival and self-esteem, I needed to take the next step— requesting information under the Freedom of Information Act.

Not that I had the faintest idea *how* to do that, but maybe the local Victim Liaison Representative, a Maj. Reynolds, could help. I gave him a call. What a contrast to Vivian Hightower in San Antonio! I'd never met the guy and after my phone conversation with him, I hoped I never would. When I asked how to request information under the Freedom of Information Act (FOIA), he was curt and unfriendly.

"Read the regulation and follow the instructions," he said.

The regulation? The instructions? And that was about all I got.

"You're supposed to help people, not make them feel like half-wits," I said.

He responded with a remark that implied, bottom line, he had better things to do, and I, of course, felt myself immediately move into hover craft mode, lasers in the strike position. Anger surged through my body, and tears pricked my eyes. Why did every step in the process have to be so difficult, like wading through thigh-deep mud that kept sucking me down?

Why couldn't he have been more helpful? Shouldn't he, as the Victim Liaison Representative, for God's sake, understand that most people have never been forced to request anything under the Freedom of Information Act? How about "let me fax you a sample?" Or "let me send you the form you are supposed to fill out"? Or something? Even a little recognition that I'm hurting would help.

I stewed for a few days and then made the difficult decision to talk to Col. Wilcott, my current commander. On the one hand, I hated to bring up the investigation so soon in my new job. On the other, I recognized that Col. Wilcott would find out sooner or later, if he didn't already know and I preferred that the information come from me, not some MP officer passing through.

This time I told my story in a much abbreviated form, adding that I wasn't happy with the service I'd received from Maj. Reynolds. Or lack of service, actually. Col. Wilcott listened sympathetically and before I knew it, he'd made an appointment to meet with the colonel in charge of the Staff Judge Advocate, the unit that supervised victim liaison work. A few days later, my commander asked me to meet with him.

"I've passed on your concerns about the lack of service," he said. "If you want to call Major Reynolds again, I think you'll find him much more helpful."

I'd already decided that one bad encounter was enough for me, but I did thank the commander for his support. Then he surprised me with his next words.

"The SJA offered to let me review information on the case. However, I want you to know that I declined."

The SJA offered to let you review the information? I was shocked and grateful. Grateful that the commander had respected my right to privacy, but shocked—and appalled—that the offer had been made. My superior could see the files on my case, but I couldn't? I had to request the information, but the Army was willing to hand it over to my boss without even telling me or checking with me? What next? Where were *my* protections?

By this time, I knew I needed to seek professional counseling to help me deal with the anger and confusion I felt. Chaplain Bennett had helped me immeasurably in San Antonio, but he was far away now. Although my experiences in the last year had left me gun-shy of military assistance, I needed *something*. So I reluctantly called the Army Medical Center to find out what kind of assistance might be available.

During that initial phone call, I chose to withhold my name.

"Who is this?" the voice on the other end of the line questioned several times.

"It's not important that you know who I am," I said, hoping that the person I was talking to would understand what a big step it was for me to even make the phone call. "I don't like the idea of there being a record in my medical file. All I want to know is, as an assault victim in the U.S. Army, where would I have to go for counseling?"

"You would have to be treated at the center's psychiatric ward."

That idea felt scary and inappropriate to me. Wouldn't the Army then be able to open my files to future commanders who might not decline to read them as Col. Wilcott had? Would I be setting myself up for further humiliation?

"Isn't there any other service available?" I asked.

"No, not unless you want to go out and find your own counselor and pay out of your own pocket."

That answer made my hair hurt. By this time I was completely exhausted emotionally, and what I wanted to do was go home and cry. Instead, as soon as I arrived at my apartment, I changed into running clothes and pounded the streets of Waikiki, hoping that if I exhausted myself physically, I'd be too tired to dream. Then, after my run, I called around for information on officiating sports events. In San Antonio, officiating had kept me too busy to think, so I decided that as soon as I returned from my scheduled trips to D.C. and the Orient, I would begin officiating again.

Then it was time for Jim's first dinner at my apartment. I remember how much effort I put into that night, preparing a special meal which I would serve on a nicely set table lighted by candles, changing into a dress and touching my skin with perfume before Jim arrived. When the doorbell rang, I was ready with a colorful lei, of course, and traditional kisses for the smartly dressed man outside my door. Then, after a toast on the lanai with a chilled bottle of Martenelli's sparkling cider, I took him on a tour of the apartment. He was impressed, or so I like to think. We ate on the lanai, watching reflections of the sunset play on the high-rises around us. A perfect evening.

No matter where we were or what we were doing, I felt so at ease with Jim. I loved to hear his laughter and to hear myself laugh with him, and I was deeply thankful for his support as I struggled with the aftermath of the investigation, for he always listened respectfully and helped me make sense of the confusion. There were no words to express how it felt to have this opportunity for us to be close for the first time, without the constraints of a long distance relationship, but I wished the magical night would last forever. That I would feel safe forever.

Unfortunately, nights away from Jim brought continued nightmares, and during the day I would occasionally start to cry for no reason. I knew I had to pursue the idea of counseling, preferably outside the Army. But my search would have to wait until after my trip to D.C. which was scheduled to begin October 9.

In my new job, which I still hold at this moment, I wear four hats for the Engineers. Provost Marshal, which deals with police liaison and law enforcement type issues; Security Manager, processing applications for security clearances; Acting Inspector General for the Pacific Ocean Division, meaning I'm the person available for employees

who need to address problems or have concerns or complaints about their jobs; and Assistant Chief of Staff, providing assistance as requested. My trip to D.C. would provide
me with inbriefs, training, and general orientation to my
responsibilities as Acting Inspector General and Provost
Marshal.

Boarding the plane for the brutal twelve hour flight
from Hawaii to D.C. was difficult. After less than two
months in Hawaii, I wasn't ready to leave yet, but I had a
job to do. In Washington I attended meetings and briefs for
three packed days. On the last day, I met with Col. Driscoll,
the Chief for Security and Law Enforcement and a military
police officer. He was a slight man with a pronounced
Boston accent and a brisk manner, the kind of officer I
would have taken to in the past. But not now. I don't know if
it was the difficulty I had meeting his bright blue eyes or
something else about my behavior that gave me away, but
we hadn't been together long when he asked me why I was
so uneasy.

"I don't like MPs," I said, surprising myself with my
bluntness.

I'm sure I surprised him as well. After all, he knew *I*
was an MP and had been for many years.

"Don't take it personally," I assured him. "When
I'm with MPs, I'm just not sure who to trust."

When I mentioned I'd had some bad experiences in
Panama, he said he'd heard about my case, confirming my
suspicions that people I'd never met probably knew as
much, if not more, than I did about the investigation.

"I can't speak for others," he said, "but I hope they
take some action on this guy."

What a comfort it was to hear support from a
member of the military police. As we talked, I explained
how frustrating the past two years had been, how helpless I
sometimes felt. When I used the word helpless, he sat a little
straighter in his chair and then showed me that his support
wasn't just meaningless words.

"There's an organization that represents women in
the military," he said. "Maybe they can help you. Give them

a call." As he spoke, he was dialing a number. Then he handed me the phone and left the room. I admit I was somewhat stunned.

"DACOWITS, Captain Serrano, can I help you?" a voice said in my ear.

"Yes...yes," I stuttered at first, unsure of what to say. "My name is Captain Fischer. I was a victim of assault, and I'm not very happy about what's happening. Is there someone I can talk to about it?"

"When are you available?" the voice asked.

"Well, I'm not from this area. I'll be returning to Hawaii tomorrow."

"We do have a representative with the Committee in Hawaii. Would you like to speak with her?"

I blinked. I'd not expected to come all the way to the East Coast to find out about a support mechanism in Hawaii, but I'd take whatever I could get.

"Yes, that will be fine," I said.

With a name—Dr. Jackie Young—and an Oahu phone number in my notebook, I hung up the phone and let Col. Driscoll know he could come on back into his office.

"Thank you so much," I said to him, thinking that sometimes God played his cards at exactly the right time. Perhaps this DACOWITS, which I learned was an acronym for Defense Advisory Committee on Women in the Services, would be able to give me the support I needed.

"Best of luck," the colonel said, and I had the feeling he really meant it.

That afternoon the flight home to Hawaii didn't seem quite as long. Not only did I have a reunion with Jim to look forward to, I'd also met an MP officer who seemed to believe me. And until I found justice, I would grab for every promise of hope I could.

The Last Straw

Back in Hawaii, I was happy to be with Jim again. Soon I became aware that even he was becoming a target for my unresolved anger. I would find myself so impatient and restless, wanting to talk to him, demanding to talk to him *now*. But when I *did* talk to him, I would avoid talking about my problems with the Army because I wanted to shut out the world that was overwhelming me and just *be* with him. I knew he had to be wondering what was really going on with me, and that I might damage our relationship if I didn't get some help.

About this time I met a woman named Pam at a luncheon. We began a casual conversation in which I learned that she had a counseling background and knew some of the psychologists at the Army Medical Center. When I mentioned that I was looking for a rape counseling program but didn't want to visit the mental ward at the hospital, she offered to make a few inquiries for me. A few days later she called me at the office.

"My counselor friend says the Army doesn't currently have a rape counseling program and that you can get a waiver to go to a clinic in downtown Honolulu," she said.

She gave me the number of the clinic and suggested I give them a call and maybe make an appointment or two, to see if the program would meet my needs. If so, the Army Medical Center would give me a waiver and pay the cost of my counseling.

I followed her suggestion, making an appointment to see a clinic counselor almost immediately. Over the course of a month, I scheduled a number of sessions. Then when I decided I would like to continue at the clinic, I contacted Pam again.

"Who do I need to see about a waiver?" I asked.

She assured me she would find out and get right back to me, but when she called me back, she had bad news.

The Army Medical Center would not give me a referral to continue my counseling at the local crisis center.

"I'm sorry to hear that," I said as calmly as I could, not wanting her to think I was ungrateful for her efforts. "Thanks for trying."

When I hung up, I lowered my head into my hands. *Nothing comes easy, Everything has to be a fight. But I can't give up.* I looked up the number of the head of psychiatry at the medical center and called. Surely the officer in charge, a high-ranking officer, could make it happen, I thought. But he couldn't. Or wouldn't.

I remember saying to him at one point in our conversation, "If someone were on top of a building ready to jump, you guys would just want to give them a push."

I couldn't understand why, when I was uncomfortable in their environment but had found counseling I trusted, they couldn't just let me go. After all, I'd been told I could get a waiver. Why had this changed?

"The information you were given was bad information," the colonel explained. "We do have a rape counseling program."

In frustration, I asked for the negative response in writing, and when I received the memo several days later, I sat down and cried. But I couldn't cry for long because my trip to the Orient was approaching, and I had lots to do before I left.

Thanksgiving Dinner was a priority. I would be in Korea on Thanksgiving Day, but Jim and I planned to celebrate early. This would be the first Thanksgiving dinner I'd ever cooked myself. A challenge! I had no idea turkeys would be so hard to come by a week before the date we'd picked to celebrate, so I ended up making do with a smoked turkey from the commissary. To avoid any other unforeseen difficulties, I planned the dinner details as carefully as a military campaign.

By the time Jim rang the doorbell, I had to have the table set, dinner ready, and myself looking like a million dollars. This meant rising early on the appointed day for a flurry of cleaning and dusting. Then I started the desserts—

chocolate cake and cherry pie. Mid-afternoon I set the table with a peach table cloth and light green place mats with matching napkins. I placed a three-tiered candelabra in the center of the table. When the table was ready, I set the coffee table for appetizers—a place mat and napkins, two glasses for our sparkling cider.

Then—pop the turkey into the oven and set the timer: pull out the basket for rolls and line it with a napkin; frost the cake; jump in the shower, but don't put on the outfit laid out on the bed—the gold leather skirt and gold silk blouse—yet. Start the side dishes first; then fix the salad and appetizers. Thirty minutes to go. The turkey, cooked to a golden brown, is done and ready to be placed on the cutting board. Time to get dressed, to fuss with my hair which doesn't always do what I want it to do. The doorbell rings, and I pop the rolls into the oven before I answer it. Whew, it was a lot of work. I'm surprised and pleased when everything turns out perfectly.

That first Thanksgiving dinner was a great success, a wonderful evening when for a time I put aside my problems. We ate and ate, talking all the time about Jim's job and my job and the softball officiating I had begun recently. I enjoyed sharing with Jim any unusual officiating situations I'd run into and appreciated his take on my questions.

Shortly before I left on my trip to Asia, my Uncle Byron called. A distant relative who was stationed in Hawaii when our family lived here, Uncle Byron lives in Alaska now, but he has a place on Molokai and he visits the Islands as often as he can. He asked if I'd visit the volcano on the Big Island with him, and we set a date to go right after I returned from Korea, Japan, and Okinawa. A weekend with Uncle Byron would be a kick!

I visited Korea first where the cold winter weather seemed brutal after the warmth of Hawaii. Soon after I arrived, I took a few vacation days and visited Chaplain Tim at Osan Air Force Base. Incredibly, or at least so it seemed for someone who had spent the last five years in Panama, Texas, and Hawaii, snow fell on Thanksgiving Day, allowing Tim and I to enjoy snowball fights followed by hot chocolate. We also made time for a little sightseeing, including a few ancient temples and some historical sites from the Korean War. Since this was my first trip to Korea, everything was new to me.

After a happy few days, I traveled back to Seoul for the business part of my trip. My contact was a Mr. Williams, the Security Manager for the Engineer District. He had visited Hawaii recently, so I recognized him when he came to pick me up at my hotel, the Dragon Hill. Outside the hotel a freezing wind chilled my face and fingers, reminding me of the days I'd pulled MP duty at West Point football games more than a decade earlier. I would never forget one particular cold Saturday. Those of us who were directing traffic knew we were in trouble when the cars coming through our gates were piled with snow, although the streets around us were bare.

"Which direction did you come from?" we anxiously asked each driver. Sure enough, within an hour inches of wet whiteness fell on us and the traffic around us, causing temporary gridlock as the roads iced over. We called for sand trucks and managed to keep control of the chaos, but it was one long, miserable day. This trip to Korea was reminding me that cold winters just weren't my favorite thing!

Fortunately, my orientation proved to be much better than the weather. I enjoyed the briefings with the Corps of Engineers staff and my tour of their headquarters. But as the time neared for my briefing with the Military Police/CID Liaison, I grew nervous. I remember sitting in Mr. William's car, wishing I could stay safely there, hoping that he did not sense my uneasiness.

Eventually, of course, I had to get out of the car and enter the MP offices. Once inside, I found myself trying not to make eye contact with anyone, just in case I recognized someone from Panama. Or they recognized me. When Mr. Williams moved away to speak to a secretary, I looked quickly at a series of pictures on the office wall—the Chain of Command here in Korea. Thank God, the only face I recognized was that of Command Sergeant Major Kinkaid, a non-commissioned officer who had left Panama six months before Lt. Col. Smith had arrived. I'd always liked Command Sgt. Maj. Kinkaid and had the strangest sense now that he would be friend rather than foe.

"May I see Command Sergeant Major Kinkaid while we are waiting for the commander?" I asked the secretary.

"I'll check for you, ma'am," she responded. A few minutes later, she was escorting me to his office.

Command Sgt. Maj. Kinkaid's friendly round face broke into a smile when he saw me, and I knew the minute he hugged me that my intuition about him had been correct.

"What are you doing here?" he asked.

I was explaining my new assignment when the secretary popped her head into the office.

"Ma'am, the commander will see you now," she said.

I left with the invitation to return as soon as I'd finished with the commander. Our meeting was just a short formality, and soon I was back in Command Sgt. Maj. Kinkaid's office, expecting we would spend some time telling golf stories and exaggerating our most recent scores. The guy was a great golfer, and we'd walked the greens together several times in Panama.

I couldn't help noticing, however, that he seemed to be having a little trouble meeting my gaze.

"What is it?" I asked.

"First, I want to say I am so sorry about your experiences in Panama after I departed," he said.

I dropped my gaze to the floor, trying to hide any hint of tears. I wasn't surprised he knew about my situation, but his kindness disarmed me. Just hearing the words "I'm sorry" from someone who obviously meant them could make me cry these days.

"Thank you for your kind words," I choked out.

He sat silently for a moment, but I could tell he had something else to say, information he thought he should share, but didn't really want to.

"Have you seen the recent promotion list for colonel?" he asked hesitantly.

"No." I had a bad feeling about this conversation.

"His name is on the list."

I thought I must have misheard Command Sgt. Maj. Kinkaid's words. "Excuse me, surely you're not telling me that Lieutenant Colonel Smith's name is on the list?"

"It is. I'm so sorry."

I stared at the uniformed man on the other side of the desk. I'd never known him to lie before, but I simply could not believe his words.

"Show me...do you have the list?" I stammered.

He pulled a sheaf of paper from the corner of his desk and pointed to a name half way down the second page. In disbelief I read the name of the man who had assaulted me in Panama. *A promotion to full colonel? How could the Army select this man for a promotion? Surely this means he hasn't had to suffer any consequences for his actions.*

I was stunned. Since the day I talked to the CID office in D.C. and heard that I wasn't to be told the outcome of my case, I'd begun to accept the fact that there would be no court martial. But a promotion? The possibility had never even crossed my mind. Never.

This news was the last straw, marking one of my lowest moments since the assault itself. It was the ultimate insult, adding more humiliation to what seemed to be a never-ending, nightmarish experience.

Reeling with Shock

"Are you okay?" Command Sgt. Maj. Kinkaid's voice interrupted my dazed shock.

"I...I don't feel very well," was the best I could do.

"Ma'am, if you have free time this evening, could we meet at seven?" Obviously he thought I shouldn't be left alone to digest the bad news. I agreed to meet him at the Red Dragon later that evening, but I needed to be—*had* to be—alone right now. Fortunately it was almost lunch time, and I asked Mr. Williams if he could return me to my hotel until our next appointment. Back in my room, I flung myself across my bed and buried my burning face in the hotel pillow.

My last appointment later this afternoon was with CID. *CID. The organization that ran the investigation. Every CID officer in the world had no doubt heard about my case.* I knew I had to keep it together.

I don't remember much about that CID meeting, but I must have survived, because soon Mr. Williams was dropping me off at the hotel.

"Thanks for everything," I said. "I'll see you in the morning." Did he know, I wondered, that I was dying inside? After he left, I wandered into a small snack bar, looking for a soft drink and place to collect my thoughts. I didn't want to believe the news I'd heard. But the minute I sat down, the reality struck me, and I felt tears building behind my eyes. I raced for my room where I tore off my uniform as if it were suffocating me and jumped into a hot shower. When I was dressed again, I lay down and cried until I drifted into a light doze.

The phone rang. "Hello, ma'am? I'm in the lobby."

I freshened up quickly and hurried down to meet Command Sgt. Maj. Kinkaid. Although I thought I might never eat again, he was hungry, so we went into the bar where he could order off the menu and I could get another coke.

"So ma'am, tell me about your work and how things are going for you in Hawaii?" he asked once we were settled.

I told him how Col. Mitchell helped me get the transfer to Hawaii and what I was doing now.

"How about you?" I asked.

"Well, you're not going to believe it, but I got married!" A sheepish grin split his face, and no wonder. In Panama, he'd been one of the most eligible bachelors on the base, with a lot of unattached women interested in him, but he'd managed to stay single.

"Congratulations," I laughed, clinking my coke can against his beer bottle. And we spent a couple of hours in cheerful conversation, repeating and embellishing stories of golfing and fishing in Panama. Before I knew it, the evening had flown by and it was time to hit the sack.

The sergeant reached over and put his hand on my shoulder. "I want you to know I think you are a great person, a good officer. Let me know if I can do anything for you."

His kindness had soothed my spirit, and I said goodbye gratefully and somewhat sadly. My trip to Korea was almost over—just one more day—but I would not soon forget my time with Command Sgt. Maj. Kinkaid or with Tim Bennett.

To my delight, my last day held one more pleasant reunion. A friend of mine, Maj. Kathy Wright, was stationed in Korea, and she and I were able to meet for dinner my last night. I had met Kathy in 1988 at the Military Police Officer Advanced Course in Fort McClellan, Alabama and immediately taken to her. She's a super officer, one I hope makes general some day, if she can stay in the war that long. We talked for hours, swapping stories and catching up on the rest of our school mates. Many were now out of the Army, others were just making the grade, and some, like Kathy, were climbing ahead.

By the time we'd been together an hour, I knew I could trust her, and I shared my Panama experience with her and confessed how, although I'd been a gung-ho soldier for years just like her, now I just wanted out. She listened thoughtfully, and I cried, savoring the temporary relief that came from getting it out of my system for the time being. When we parted, we promised to stay in touch. One thing I've discovered in the past few years: when people you know learn the details, you find out who your real friends are!

I arrived in Okinawa late the next afternoon and was greeted by my host Maj. Brown. It could be tough trying to find someone you'd never met before, but in this case, only one person—a lanky, dark man—waited outside the gate, so I figured he must be Maj. Brown. He welcomed me to Okinawa and escorted me to the guest house where I would be staying during my stay.

As soon as I was settled in my room, I picked up the phone. "Do you have a listing for Dan Knight?" I asked the military operator.

I knew that Dan and Julie Knight, my sponsor family from Panama, were now stationed in Okinawa, and I'd written them a note saying that I'd try to visit them. Julie picked up the phone after two rings, and I smiled at the excitement in her familiar voice.

"Linda! Great to hear from you. We'll come get you and you can have dinner with us. The kids will be so surprised!"

Two hours later, I was in the Knight's comfortable living room, listening to the sound of two teenagers coming home from school, calling to their mother before they even got in the door.

"Mom, what are we having for dinner tonight?"

Then they were inside, their eyes widening with surprise when they saw me, their hugs putting a grin on my face. We ordered pizza for dinner, which pleased them mightily, and gabbed and chattered non-stop until they went off to do their homework.

Julie and I had skirted the topic of Lt. Col. Smith while the kids were in the room, but I knew we wouldn't avoid it forever. I knew that CID had questioned Julie during their investigation, and the fact that I'd never told her what was going on during our days in Panama had often bothered me. Especially when I'd had the feeling she knew way back then that *something* was wrong.

"I'm so sorry," I said now. "I never meant for you to find out through an official investigation."

With their years of experience on military bases, Julie and Dan could understand my original reasons for staying mum about the assault and assured me I didn't need to feel guilty about not clueing them in earlier. But the CID call *had* surprised them.

"Did you get a chance to tell them about the times the commander would call your house looking for me?" I asked. Although I'd never told the whole story to Julie, she'd known that I often felt hounded by Lt. Col. Smith.

"Unfortunately, no," she said. "When CID called me, they only asked me a few questions that didn't give me the opportunity to volunteer all the information I had."

I was sorry to hear that, but I didn't allow my disappointment to put a damper on our visit. Over the next few days, I saw the family again several times. During the day, I attended the required briefings and site visits, of course, but in the evening I enjoyed being with the Knights. The kids—now two senior high girls and junior high boy since the oldest had gone off to college—told me all about school and sports and their lives. When it was time to leave Okinawa, Julie offered to take me to the airport. She picked me up early enough so we could have lunch together first—no Dan, no kids—in a great little tempura place. We talked more about the events in Panama, and her support encouraged me. Many, if not most, MP personnel probably believed I was a liar, and that hurt, but I knew now there were good people everywhere who believed me.

Later that day I arrived in Japan and was chauffeured to a guesthouse not far from the headquarters for the Japan Engineer District. I spent the next few days in briefings and visits to the IG, Military Police, and CID. Once again, meeting with MPs and with the CID staff was difficult for me. I couldn't help but wonder what the person across the desk knew, what he thought, whether or not he was a good friend of Lt. Col. Smith. Maybe I was being paranoid. After all, there are hundreds of MP officers in the service. But having been one myself for over twelve years, I knew how small the military police world was. I knew how quickly news flew, not just around a base, but sometimes around the world.

Despite my nervousness, I gathered my courage and asked the CID Commander for information on requesting copies of files. I didn't tell him *why* I was asking, of course, and for all I know, he may have picked up the phone the minute I left his office and called Lt. Col. Smith on the East Coast to report that I was up to something. But I figured I had nothing to lose, and he couldn't very well withhold this kind of information from me. So I left his office with the number and address of the Records Holding Center for CID tucked in my notebook.

Now I was more than ready to go home. Seeing my friends in Korea and Okinawa had been great, but my nights had been restless during the entire trip, so I was exhausted. And the news about the commander's promotion had brought my anger back up to the boiling point. When I was alone in my room, I cried a lot, unable to find any other release for my feelings. I just wanted to go home.

At the Volcano's Edge

Back in Honolulu again, I slept unbelievably well. Despite my continuing agitation over the news of Lt. Col. Smith's selection for promotion, there was something comforting about being home, about sleeping in my own bed, and being able to call Jim. However, I hardly had time to check in at the office before I took another trip—this time a vacation trip to the Big Island of Hawaii with my Uncle Byron.

Uncle Byron is a "pistol", to coin a phrase I've learned from Jim. Although he has thickened through the middle since those early years, he's still the adventurous guy he's always been. He and my dad used to scuba dive together, and I'll never forget a close call they had one day when a treacherous current separated them. Each dropped his gear and headed for the shore, not knowing what had happened to the other. When my dad reached the shore, he called the Coast Guard and reported Uncle Byron missing. Miles down the beach, Uncle Byron was reporting Dad missing. Although the two friends were cheerfully reunited later that day, my mom was worried for awhile and what a relief it was to hear that Dad was alive. To this day, I won't scuba dive.

I hadn't seen Uncle Byron for over ten years and was looking forward to getting to know the Big Island through his eyes. We flew over on a Saturday morning, and after renting a car, he gave me a quick tour of scenic areas near the airport.

At one point, we crossed a bridge and viewed a lava tube with a stream running through it. The stream emptied into a small pond before continuing on toward the ocean below. When we stopped the car and waded up through the short tube, we were awestruck by the sight on the other side—a gorgeous valley with mountains rising steeply to the sky. We promised each other we would come back and hike up the valley someday, but for now we continued on, not stopping again until we spotted a rushing waterfall. All along the way, the beauty of the Big Island, the largest and youngest of the Hawaiian chain, was more spectacular than words could describe.

After our drive, we headed into a small town to pick up a few odds and ends, bottled water, candy bars, and an offering for Pele the Fire Goddess. We planned to visit Kilauea, Hawaii's active volcano, late in the evening and according to tradition, would leave an offering to ensure our safety. Byron selected the traditional bottle of gin; I picked out a small bottle of wine—choices we believed Madame Pele would appreciate. Then we drove to a bed-and-breakfast nestled in the peace and quiet of the mountainside.

We took a little time to settle into our comfortable rooms, and I checked out the Jacuzzi because I knew I'd want to relax in warm, bubbling water after the trek we planned for that evening. Then I stuffed my backpack with bottled water, a small pen-type flashlight, a camera, and the gifts for Madame Pele and off we went, stopping only to pick up dinner because we didn't expect to return until well after the 9:00 p.m. dinner service closing.

The sun was setting, and I was excited about seeing the volcano, expecting an evening of adventure. Little did I imagine, however, just *how* adventurous the next hours would be!

By the time we parked near the ranger trailer, darkness had fallen. Adjusting our eyes to the dark, we walked towards a field of black where a few couples stood behind a roped area and peered into the distance. The bright red glow with clouds of steam rising as the lava hit the sea looked to be only a few miles away.

I followed Uncle Byron's lead as he ducked under the rope and headed toward the distant glow. Although I could still feel the heat from the sun on the black lava rock, I was glad for the blue mechanic's jumper I wore over shorts and tee-shirt. On my feet were sturdy thick-leather hiking boots. Uncle Byron wore shorts and tennis shoes. He didn't carry any water as he had done this many times before, but I wasn't going anywhere without water!

We hadn't gone far when Uncle Byron said, "You may feel drafts of hot air shoot up from the ground, Linda. It's from the lava underground, so don't let it scare you."

The hot drafts didn't scare me, but something else did.

"What's that sound?" I heard liquid flowing somewhere. Uncle Byron heard nothing so we continued on. The sound came again, stopping me in my tracks. I had this terrifying vision of fiery lava flowing like a river right below my feet.

"Do you hear that?"

"What?"

"That sound. The sound of liquid flowing. I'm not going anywhere!"

"Trust me, Linda. You're safe here. I'll let you know if it gets dangerous."

Uncle Byron finally convinced me, and we started forward again. The next time I heard the sound, I realized where it came from and started to laugh.

"What's so funny?" he asked.

I hated to admit how dumb I'd been, but I had to tell him that what I'd been hearing was nothing more than water sloshing in the bottle in my backpack.

We had slipped under the rope at about 7:00 p.m. Now it was close to 10:00 p.m., and in the cool air, I was glad I'd worn the jumpsuit. I was also grateful for my boots, because hiking through lava fields in the dark is rough, and the toes of my boots banged frequently into unseen rocks. Although the rock was hard, in some places its surface made a crackling sound as we walked over it.

"Be careful," Uncle Byron said. "When lava breaks into small pieces, it can cut you like slivers of glass."

The landscape was uneven and full of small hills and valleys where the lava had cooled. As we climbed up and over huge buckles of rock, we soon found that our small flashlights were worthless and began to rely on the brightness of the full moon to light the way.

"Hey, how much farther?" I asked, aware that the glow didn't seem much closer.

"I don't know. It's farther than I expected. Let's give it another hour and then head back."

About this time, we reached an area along the beach. The formations resulting from the mix of water and lava were grotesque and fascinating. When I found a small glass fishing float, I pulled off my backpack and placed it carefully inside. It would be a souvenir of the trip.

At 11:00 p.m., we decided we had gone far enough. I took pictures of the red glow and clouds of smoke which appeared closer than when we'd started, but still far enough away that I felt safe. Opening up the gin and wine, we toasted Pele by pouring the contents of the bottle on the beach and lava.

"I don't feel too well," Byron said suddenly. "I think the fumes are making me sick."

I broke out the water for him before we headed out in the opposite direction. This time I took the lead. I was hungry and could hear the bubbles in the Jacuzzi calling my name. Every so often, however, I asked if we were headed in the right direction. After all, Uncle Byron was the expert.

"Yeah, yeah," he said, sounding sicker now.

We slowed down so that Uncle Byron could gulp water whenever he needed it.

Although I felt good and could have moved at a faster clip, I began to worry about my hiking companion. If I had to leave him and go for help, how would I ever find him again in the dark? All I could see was black ahead of us.

"Wait," he exclaimed.

This is it. I'll have to go for help. How did we get ourselves into this? I returned to the spot where he was resting.

"Look!" he said with excitement.

All I could see was the dark gray of the lava. Was he becoming delirious? Then I saw small swirls of smoke rising from the ground about twenty-five feet away. When we moved closer to the smoke, we could see a red glow under the ground's surface and feel its heat. The adrenaline in my veins started pumping. The heat prevented us from getting any closer, so we stopped and marveled at the sight before us.

Fiery liquid rock oozed from the ground. I had a few pennies, and I tossed them into the flowing lava, expecting them to disappear as they would if I'd tossed them into water. Instead, I heard them clink and saw them bounce as if they were hitting concrete before they finally melted into the red glow. I took out my camera and squatted as close as I could, feeling the heat on my legs. After a quick "Kodak moment", I was ready to move on. Being this close made me feel the power of the flowing lava.

This time Uncle Byron took the lead, after deciding that we needed to go around the lava field in front of us. That sounded good to me, and I stayed close behind him as he moved out. Suddenly he stopped so quickly that I almost stepped on his heels.

"What?" I asked.

Then I looked down and blinked. I was standing on a piece of rock about two feet square with ragged edges and a 1 inch crack all around it. Molten lava glowed redly through the crack.

"Holy cow," I said, not moving an inch.

"Go back," Uncle Byron barked. Believe me, I obeyed that order, stepping over the crack and heading back in the direction we had come. My uncle was on my heels.

"We'll have to make a bigger circle," he said when we were out of harm's way.

By now it was after midnight, and Uncle Byron wasn't feeling any better. Each time I felt a gust of warm air from between the lava rocks, I moved with a greater sense of urgency. Shortly before 2:00 in the morning, we reached a ridge that was about forty feet high.

"Hey" I said. "Why don't we take a break?" I suggested, handing him the water bottle.

Watching him tip the contents of the large bottle into his mouth, I felt a new uneasiness. We should have brought more water. I took one gulp before replacing the bottle in my backpack. From now on, we'd have to conserve water.

"I'm going to climb to the top of this ridge. Maybe I'll see a light or something for us to walk towards," I said, remembering that the ranger trailer had a light.

As I climbed, I felt the razor sharpness of the lava rock tearing into my hands, and I pulled my sleeves down as far as I could to protect them. The lava shredded the cloth like paper. I moved slowly up the cliff carefully placing each step before reaching up. A fall could be treacherous. But I wasn't careful enough. When I saw a round dark spot, I was so convinced it was firm ground I stepped out—and found myself falling into darkness.

Fortunately, the hole was only about five feet deep and I was able to pull myself up and out without too much damage. Too bad I'd never thought to bring gloves, I thought, trying to ignore the fact that my hands were burning from the small slivers of rock working their way into my skin.

When I reached the top of the ridge, I hollered down to Uncle Byron. He didn't answer, so I sat down and scooted over the rocks to get closer to the edge. Big mistake! Rock slivers pushed through the jumpsuit and through the shorts, pricking my bottom. I scooted no more and strained my eyes trying to make out a human form below me. Nothing. I could see only a blackness. Again I yelled Uncle Byron's name into the darkness and this time I heard his response.

"Walk along the ridge, Linda. I'll find my way up."

After he made his way up, we crept along the ridge for about thirty minutes. By now it was 4 a.m. and we were exhausted. When we reached an area where the lava rock was covered with tall grass, we sat down so that Uncle Byron could finish the little water we had left. He said he would be all right, he just felt sick to his stomach and needed to rest, but I insisted that we stop for the night.

We lay down in the tall grass. The night air felt cold, the sweat I had worked up worked against me now. So I pulled grass over me for warmth. Both of us managed to doze for an hour or two. When the sun made its way into the sky, we awoke and saw that our ridge was only about a quarter mile from the ranger trailer and our car. We plodded down to safety.

"I remember getting lost last time," Uncle Byron admitted when we neared the car.

I tried a little sarcastic humor. "Now *that* would have been good to know before we started!"

We never ate the steak and shrimp with baked potatoes that had spent the night in the trunk of the car, and I never sat in the bubbling water of the Jacuzzi. Instead, we only had time for a shower and breakfast at the B and B. The shower's hot water stung the lava rock cuts and slivers embedded in my skin, but breakfast tasted great! By the time we headed for the airport, Uncle Byron was feeling better, which relieved me immensely. And then it was time to part. I told him I looked forward to his next visit, but it wouldn't be to a volcano!

In fact, I doubt I will ever visit the volcano again. I know now that we shouldn't have slipped under that rope without letting someone know, but it's more than physical danger that keeps me from a return visit to Kilauea. That red molten lava would serve to remind me of the volcanic rage I had carried inside for so long. The lava's destructive power would remind me of how rage and a sense of helplessness can eat away at self-esteem. At some point during our dark night on the mountain, I had realized that finding a way to safety had to become a priority. As it is now.

It's Christmas Time!

When I returned to the office on Monday, I knew what I had to do. I made an appointment to see the commander later that afternoon. Then I called the Records Holding Center, using the number I'd been given by the CID commander in Japan, and asked for the address I needed to request my files. Looking at the address on the yellow pad on my desk, I started to cry. By now everyone in the MP community would have seen the promotion list. Those who knew about my case would naturally assume that, since the Army was rewarding Lt. Col. Smith with the rank of full colonel, there had been no truth to my accusations. They would think I was a liar. Once again, humiliation swept through me.

That afternoon I met with the commander in his office. Our first order of business was to discuss my Far East trip, but I know he could tell something was wrong.

"What else can I help you with?" he asked, after I shared my trip experiences with him.

I wanted to be honest with him. "I don't know if you can help me, sir, but I should tell you that I saw the recent promotion list for colonel. I just can't believe *he* is on the list, sir. They must not have done anything to him."

The commander's look of dismay and concern told me I didn't need to use names.

"What can I do to help?" he asked again.

"Sir, I don't think you can do anything, but I want you to know what I would like to do. I have the number and address for the Records Holding Center for CID, and I plan to request the case file so I can find out the disposition of the case. I'm not sure what will happen next. This is just my worst nightmare come true."

The commander offered his help once again, and I was grateful that he at least listened to me. However, back in my office, I faced the possibility that no one in the system could do much for me anymore. I'd have to take care of myself. I was gazing out the window when a voice interrupted my thoughts.

"Ma'am?" Sgt. Nakamura, the Military Personnel Noncommissioned Officer, stood in the door.

I came back to the present. "Yes? What can I do for you, Sgt. Nakamura?"

"Have you thought about where you would like to have the party—you getting promoted and all—or who will do the pinning?"

In less than three weeks, my promotion to major would come through which, in Army tradition, calls for lots of celebrating. Traditionally, the officer who gets promoted hosts a party or get-together at the officers' club. But the moment I'd worked toward for so many years now felt tarnished by the events of the last two years. I knew I wouldn't throw a club party.

"Sorry, no party," I said. Then, seeing his face fall in disappointment, I added, "But I do want to have a buffet laid out after the ceremony in the general's office. And my parents will be here, so my dad can share pinning honors with the commander."

The sergeant grinned, "Sounds like a winner to me, ma'am. I'll take care of the ceremony part."

I couldn't help but notice during the next few weeks that everyone in the office was more excited about the upcoming celebration than I was. I knew this would be my last promotion, all earlier hopes of making lieutenant colonel having evaporated in the past year since I reported the assault. And I didn't feel very proud of the uniform I wore anymore. Sometimes it felt more like prison garb. Only why was I doing the time instead of the guy who did the crime? I hoped I could hang in until retirement so that my pension wouldn't be lost along with all my other dreams. Hanging in there would be rough, I knew, considering that most of the time I felt ready to explode.

But the holidays were approaching, and I vowed to take a breather from the pain and trauma of the past. After all, Jim and I would be spending our first Christmas together since 1990, and then my parents would be arriving for the promotion ceremony. Between now and then, I had lots to do—both for Christmas and for the ceremony.

Fortunately, the staff at work was a great bunch and did a lot to buoy my spirits. The two secretaries, Samantha and Maria, went all out decorating the office and bringing in Christmas goodies. I helped by sacrificing myself to test their goodies. After all, somebody had to do it! And I set up my boom box to play holiday music—preferably Jingle Bell Rock, which is my favorite.

Christmas party time began, and we moved from office to office to celebrate with as many people in the division as we could. Unfortunately, we couldn't make every single party. One afternoon I wandered around the offices of the Resources Management Section staff, enjoying cookies and pop and meeting people.

"Have you met this bunch?" a secretary asked, steering me over to a small group of people sitting in one corner.

"Not yet," I said with a smile.

Even after everyone introduced themselves, I would probably not have remembered names or faces, if a slight middle-aged Hawaiian man hadn't jumped to his feet and offered me his chair.

"My name is Jeff," he said. "Here, why don't you sit by Debbie?"

"So how do you like Hawaii, Captain Fischer?" asked Debbie, a young blonde woman whom I later learned worked in funds accountability.

"I love it here," I said. "The weather is beautiful and I like getting out and seeing the island."

Jeff grinned at me. "So you're managing to find your way around okay?"

"Well, since I started officiating sports activities, I've had a little trouble finding some places. Directions can be tricky. Someone tells me 'You go to Lukuolanimakalapa Street and turn onto Mukolakalani Place.' All I want to know is—is it near Sears?"

The whole group started laughing, but Jeff and

Debbie especially seemed to appreciate my humor. Later, as I made my rounds thanking people for their hospitality and wishing them a Merry Christmas, Debbie and Jeff asked if I would join them for lunch the following week. I accepted, and so a valuable friendship was born.

Shortly after that, I met another person who was destined to become a good friend. Now that I was getting back into pretty good shape, I signed up for two local sporting activities—one called the Christmas Biathlon and the other the Jingle Bell Run—both scheduled for the same Saturday. The biathlon was a swim/run team event, which I had agreed to participate in with Michelle, a woman who worked in the legal offices downstairs from me. She was a strong swimmer; I would do the running.

Early Saturday morning, Michelle and I met to plan our strategy at Ala Moana Beach Park where the event was held. It was a beautiful day, not too hot for a good race, and soon we were gathering at the beach for the start of the race. Bang! The swimmers were off. With so many bodies splashing in the water, I had trouble keeping my eyes on Michelle, but as she neared the finish line, I spotted her and jogged to the spot where she would leave the water. Soon she tagged me, and I sped off at a fast clip. Although it wasn't long before I felt like I had a sucking chest wound, I fixed my eyes on a runner in front of me. Before I knew it, I had passed that runner, and I decided to pick off the next one. Soon that runner was behind me as well. But when I tried to catch the next one in front of me, my chest wound practically exploded, convincing me that I'd better resign myself to an easier pace. Near the finish line, my competitive spirit kicked in and I couldn't resist a brief sprint. Whew! Over the line! I'd made it!

Michelle met me at the finish line with my sweatshirt, and we talked about whether or not we should attend the awards ceremony.

"Nah," Michelle said. "I don't think we won anything. I'm taking off." And she headed for her car.

Although I felt somewhat deserted, I decided to check out the awards ceremony. I was standing alone in the crowd when a lean, dark-skinned woman looked at me and said to her companion, "She was in front of me."

When I looked behind me to see who they meant, the woman chuckled. She'd been talking about me. We introduced ourselves, and I learned her name was Becky.

"You'll win something," she predicted.

"I don't think so," I said. "We were moving pretty slow."

"What age group are you in?" she asked.

"The old ladies age group!"

"You did win," she insisted. "You finished in front of me, and we're in that group as well."

Sure enough, when they called out the winners for females 30 to 39, our team had taken second place. I wanted to celebrate my victory even though Michelle had left, so I asked Becky and her friends if I could join them for breakfast. Although I don't remember three of the women, Becky and I hit it off immediately. I learned she was a manicurist which prompted me to hide my hands under the table (I hadn't had my nails done in ages), and when we parted, Becky gave me her card. Since that time, she's fixed my nails and been my friend.

That same evening, I planned to join a few people from the executive office at the Jingle Bell Run, one of downtown Honolulu's most colorful Christmas rituals. At the time I had no idea what I was in for! I never did link up with the office group because of the crowd, but I had a great time anyway. The Jingle Bell Run is a "run" in name only, because not that many people actually run. Most walk the course, enjoying the spectacular lights and decorations on city and state buildings along the way. To add to the color, many of the entrants wear wonderful costumes. That evening I saw lots of Santas and elves. And there were even dogs decorated with bells and hooked to sleighs—the closest you can get to reindeers in the Islands! What a great tradition.

All this Christmas cheer—the parties and special events—was just what I needed for it kept me in touch with the goodness of life at a time when the turmoil and anger of dealing with the Army system might have been overwhelming. I remembered that God promises we won't have burdens or hardship "too great to bear," and so it seemed He must have had a hand in the timing of these events. While I didn't know when or how my war with the Army would end, I did know that I needed to separate it as much as possible from the life I had to live. I knew that I needed to enjoy life as much as possible. Christmas made that easier.

Meanwhile, despite their attention to holiday activities, the great staff at my office found time to take care of details for my promotion ceremony which would occur just three days after Christmas. Sgt. Nakamura made good on his promise to get the narration ready for my dad and the commander, and the two secretaries helped plan the refreshment menu. They are "make it happen" people, and by the time I left my office on December 23, the only thought in my mind was "It's Christmas time!"

I love the holiday season. I decorated my lanai railings with lights and put up a tree in my living room—a small tree but beautiful with decorations from years gone by and from places I've been during my years in the Army. Some of my most precious possessions are the ornaments that my sister and I painted as children, but I also buy something new or different every year to add to my collection. And I love arranging gifts under the tree and stuffing stockings. It's amazing that no matter how old we get, wrapping and opening presents seems to bring out the child in all of us.

On this Christmas I pulled the table in from the lanai; we would eat indoors so that I could use an elegant candelabra. We would dine on a tossed salad, thick steaks, baked potatoes, steamed green beans, and hard rolls. For dessert there would be chocolate cake with chocolate frosting. Jim strolled up right on time, dressed fashionably for the occasion and with gifts in hand. After we enjoyed a tender kiss, I took the gifts from him and placed them under the tree. Then we sipped on a sparkling non-alcoholic wine while Christmas music filled the room. Through the glass doors to the lanai, we could see colors from the last rays of sunlight dance on surrounding buildings.

When dinner was ready, we sat down to the soft glow of the candles and to the cheer that good food and good company can bring. Both Jim and I had old Christmas stories to share with each other, and the evening flew. After dinner I made myself scarce in the kitchen, so Jim could stuff my stocking, and then we opened our gifts. I loved the stocking stuffers, fun little toys and gadgets, candies and more. But Jim also surprised me with other great gifts, including Starsight for the TV and perfume.

I always have a hard time buying his presents. What do you buy a guy who has everything? But he seemed pleased with the clothes and cologne and nicely framed photos I had selected. Thoughts of our first Christmas together here in Hawaii many years ago flooded my mind, and I realized that what made this Christmas so special was knowing I would not be leaving in just a few days. I had that warm feeling of being home.

Making Major

I was still full of Christmas cheer when my parents arrived a few days later. How excited I was as I rushed off to the airport. I stopped first for a couple of leis, of course, for it wouldn't be right to let them step off the plane without the traditional aloha greeting. As the passengers deplaned, I craned my neck to catch a glimpse of a familiar face. There! I spotted my dad's silver hair and rushed forward all smiles and leis, draping a tea leaf lei around Dad's neck and beautiful carnations and rose buds around Mom's. As the flowers' fragrance filled the air, I felt sorry for the other people coming off the plane with their sad puppy "where's my lei?" faces.

I drove the scenic view into Waikiki, so that my parents could watch the waves crashing on the beach before they arrived at the apartment. They were suitably impressed, but even more so when they saw the view from my apartment. I never tire of it myself, so I'm not surprised when others are taken with it. Dad particularly enjoyed watching the young people paddling canoes in the Ala Wai Canal.

That afternoon, after we all enjoyed the mango sauce ribs at Duke's on the beach, we took a trip back into nostalgia. Dad wanted to see Schofield Barracks where he had been stationed so many years earlier, so we drove out to the middle of the island. Although the building he'd worked in was gone, he recognized some of the places on base. Then we headed back to find the townhouse we had lived in during his tour here. At the time, the area—known as Mililani—was brand new, set among the sugar and pineapple fields that have now largely disappeared. The high school that I attended had just been built and didn't have a track yet. Instead, we ran around a trail out in a field behind the locker rooms.

When we drove into Mililani, my parents commented on the changes they saw—all the high rises and

highways and miles of housing that hadn't been there earlier.
We passed the high school, now a massive complex with a
stadium sitting in the field I once ran around. Would we be
able to find our old home? As we pulled onto Anania Drive,
things started to look familiar. The recreation center we had
enjoyed so much was still standing across the street, and
there was our townhouse. Dad and Mom couldn't get over
how small it seemed, especially compared to their home in
Texas.

For the end of our drive down memory lane, we
went to Haleiwa on the North Shore for a shave ice with a
scoop of vanilla ice cream in the bottom. Polishing off the
cool refreshing delight, we all agreed that the shave ice
store—and its shave ice—had stood the test of time. Then,
after Mom and Dad had wandered through the gift shops for
awhile, we headed back to Waikiki for the night's big
event—Jim's first meeting with my parents.

They had heard about him for years, of course, and I
had no doubt they would like him, but I was a nervous
wreck by the time we were seated together at Nick's
Fishmarket, a local restaurant. The questions came fast and
furious. "Jim, tell us about what you do. How long have you
been here? What did you do in the military?" Fortunately,
Dad didn't tell any embarrassing "When Linda was a little
kid" stories; I never knew what he might pull out of his hat.
After Jim left us, my parents showered me with accolades,
letting me know they really liked Jim, and I breathed a sigh
of relief. I guess it doesn't matter how old you are, parents
meeting a boyfriend for the first time is a big deal!

The next day was December 28, the day of my
promotion ceremony. As I dressed in the uniform we call B's
(a dark green skirt and light green blouse for women),
I could hear Mom making coffee in the kitchen and Dad
chatting with her. It was so good to have them with me for
this special event. I remembered how Dad had always been
there when I was ready to cash in my chips and try something new.

"Give it sixty days," he would say. "If things don't
get better, you know you are always welcome at home."

And somehow things would always get better and so here I was, getting promoted to major. When I first joined the Army, my plans were "three years and out." But every time I thought about leaving, there had been a promotion around the corner, a school to attend, or a new assignment that kept me in the game. Now, however, I *really* wanted out. But only if I could find a way to go with dignity and respect. I was not going to fold my hand like a quitter. And I was not going to let the events of the past two years ruin this day. This was the first and last promotion ceremony my parents would attend in my career as an Army officer, and in my heart, today was more for them than for me.

At the office, I proudly introduced people to my parents and then took them to my office until Col. Wilcott came to meet them. He and my father went over a few instructions to prepare them for the moment when they would each place a gold leaf on one of my shoulders. As a lieutenant and a captain, I had worn bars on each shoulder. Now I would receive the major's gold leaf. It broke my heart to think that this was as far as I would go. It galled me to know that Harold Smith had been selected to wear the eagle of the full bird colonel despite what he had done to me.

After Jim arrived and graced me with a beautiful lei, we walked down to the commander's office where a small gathering of guests filled the room. I stood erect between my Dad and Col. Wilcott, trying to ignore the mixed emotions surging through me. I was nervous and checked for the notecard I'd slipped into my pocket just in case I forgot the words I planned to say. And I was a little sad, too, realizing how elated and proud I might have been in different circumstances.

Col. Wilcott opened the ceremony with a warm welcome and introduced my parents and Jim as our distinguished guests. Then Sgt. Nakamura took his cue from Col Wilcott's nod and said, "Attention to orders, this is to certify that the President of the United States has reposed special trust and confidence in the patriotism, valor, fidelity, and abilities of Linda A. Fischer. In view of these qualities and her demonstrated potential for increased responsibility, she is therefore promoted to the rank of Major in the United States Army."

While my Dad and Col. Wilcott placed the gold leaves on my shoulders, the words "trust and confidence" echoed painfully in my mind. Lt. Col. Smith violated that trust and confidence. Today I certainly did not have much trust and confidence in the organization I served.

But now the guests were cheering and clapping, and the ceremony continued. Col. Wilcott turned to face me, "Major Fischer," he began and I liked the sound of my new title, "Please raise your right hand and state the oath."

"I, Linda A. Fischer, having been appointed an officer in the United States Army to the rank of Major, do solemnly swear that I will support and defend the Constitution of the United States, against all enemies, foreign and domestic, that I will bear true faith and allegiance to the same; that I take this obligation freely, without any mental reservation or purpose of evasion; and that I will well and faithfully discharge the duties of the office upon which I am about to enter, so help me God."

Then it was time for my dad to say a few words. "I actually volunteered to say something here, and for a warrant officer that's extremely hard. It was important for me to know how long I had to speak because if I had five minutes, I would need two months to prepare, if I had fifteen minutes, I would need one month, and if I had two hours, I was ready right now."

Laughter broke out around the room, and I had to grin, too. But my dad's next words brought moisture to my eyes.

"I started out in the Army in 1956 and retired in 1977," he said. "During that time, I had a lot of proud moments, but this is by far the proudest for me. Thank you."

Wow! I wondered how I could possibly follow that, but then I felt the energy in the room and the buzz of excitement that always pervades promotion ceremonies wash over me.

"I'd like to thank all of you for coming to the ceremony today," I began. Then I turned and faced my parents and Jim. "This is a special day for me because never before has my family been able to share in the events that have marked my career. To have Jim and my mother and father here makes the moment all the more memorable for me. Especially my father. He has been there for me during the tough times sharing his wisdom and offering his support. A long time ago, when I graduated from high school, my dad said, 'Linda, you should think about joining the Army.' I said, 'I don't want to join the Army, Dad.' 'Okay,' he said, 'just promise me you'll go talk to them.' 'Okay,' I said. So I went down to the office, and there were two people sitting in the office—a male and a female recruiter. 'Is this the Army recruiting office?' I asked. 'Yes,' they said in unison. 'Well, you have a good day,' I said and left the office. I had fulfilled my obligation to my dad to talk to them.

"Little did I know three and a half years later when I walked back into that office that those same two recruiters would be sitting there. They both remembered me. 'Hey, didn't you walk in here about three years ago, say hello and walk back out?' 'Yes,' I answered. 'We've been looking for you,' they said.

"I started in the Army out of college and I thought three years and I'll be back in Georgetown doing something else, and here I am thirteen years later a major. It was my father who prompted me to go to OCS, and it was the best decision I could have made at the time. I attribute my success to the attributes my parents taught me over the years—to be honest and accept responsibility for my actions. I also want to thank my grandma for what I learned from her when in her care while my father was in Vietnam and my mother who kept me in line. And Jim, who is my best friend and who has been supportive of me over the years.

"There are so many people I would like to thank who are not here, those first sergeants and soldiers of the units I commanded. Their success is my success. To the leaders who provided me guidance and the opportunity to excel over the years. Finally, I'd like to thank Col. Wilcott and all of you for the opportunity to serve as a part of this

organization, and I look forward to my future with the Corps
of Engineers."

There. I'd said what I wanted to say, and it was
good to remember that in spite of Lt. Col. Smith's behavior,
there were many other soldiers—both superiors and subordinates—whom I could honestly thank.

Sgt. Nakamura took over. "Thank you for attending
today's ceremony," he said. "Please stay and join Major
Fischer and her family for the celebration lunch here in the
executive wing."

With that everyone filed by and offered their congratulations, while the ladies slipped out to prepare the
buffet lunch. My parents presented me with an elegant desk
set of dark green marble—a pyramid shaped clock, name
plate, and pen stand. It would add a classy touch to my
office. Then we gathered around tables in the office area and
dug into oyster sauce chicken, beef and broccoli, noodles,
rice, and more followed by a large cake with which the
office secretaries had surprised me. The Hawaiian word
"ohana" means family, and at lunch that day I experienced
the islands' true ohana spirit.

After we had stuffed ourselves to the gills, the party
broke up. Jim went back to work along with most of the
other guests, Samantha and Marie volunteered to clean up,
and my parents and I headed back to my apartment for an
afternoon nap. Later we strolled through Waikiki, content to
take it easy after the morning's excitement. At day's end, I
had the satisfaction of knowing that my parents were proud
of me, that my dad in particular had enjoyed every minute of
my promotion ceremony. I knew I would always remember
this day with pride.

The next few days went by too quickly while we
happily played tourist in Hawaii. I took my parents to my
favorite restaurants, and we ate a lot more than we needed
to. We spent one entire day at the Polynesian Cultural
Center, driving up the island's windward side via the scenic
route. Along the way, we stopped frequently and drank in
the breathless views of waves crashing on the shores. Every
time I take this drive, I know I never want to leave Hawaii.

One of Oahu's most impressive attractions, the Polynesian Cultural Center includes information, shows, exhibits, and activities about most of the major Pacific islands. One day is too short to see and do everything, but we covered as much ground as possible. And to be honest, the best part of the visit for me was capturing on film Mom and Dad trying to hula. Their performance convinced me that they would *not* be the main attraction at the evening show! This show, which followed a sumptuous luau and then a relaxing boat ride, was more spectacular than I can describe.

Another night Jim joined us for dinner at Buzz's Steak House, a restaurant that Mom and Dad had frequented years earlier. Once again, my parents were surprised at the changes, this time in Pearl City where the restaurant was, and kept marveling at all the new buildings. I'd been a kid during our tour here and hadn't much noticed buildings. Fun and sun was what I remembered—swimming at the pool across the street and running through the pineapple fields.

On New Year's Eve day, my parents did their final shopping. Dad wanted a fish display for the house and Mom bought shirts and other small gifts to take home to the relatives. It was late afternoon when we returned to the apartment so we could rest up for the evening's festivities. Jim was treating us to the magic show at the Hilton Hawaiian Village. What a show! I sat open-mouthed most of the time, in total awe. I've never figured out how magicians do even the simplest of tricks.

By the time we headed back to my apartment, we could already hear the occasional pops of firecrackers going off in the distance. We sat on the lanai in the cool breeze and chatted while the flurries of sound increased. When midnight grew near, I retrieved champagne and sparkling grape juice from the refrigerator and set it on the table. Now fireworks were exploding against the backdrop of mountains. And then it was midnight. We hugged and kissed and toasted each other as 1996 made its entrance, and I hoped that the New Year would bring me both serenity and justice.

New Year's Day was the last day of my parents'

visit, and we spent it fittingly with one final visit to
Hanauma Bay, a spot they had always loved. Although Dad
wasn't scuba diving anymore, he had a chance to snuba, a
water sport that allows you to breathe through an air hose
without having to wear heavy scuba gear. Mom and I soaked
up sun rays until it was time to hurry back to the apartment.
In no time at all, we were at the airport, walking to the gate
where their plane would load. Jim was there to say his good-
byes, too, and I was glad for his comforting arm around my
shoulder.

As she always does whenever we part, Mom blessed
me. This practice began many years ago when her mom, my
Grandma Valdez, was still alive. Before leaving for basic
training, I had stopped off to see Grandma, a faithful Catholic, and she had blessed me with holy water, making the sign
of the cross on my face as she whispered in the name of the
Father, the Son, and Holy Spirit. I felt she had given me a
powerful spiritual gift, and after that I never left
Georgetown until she had blessed me. Unfortunately, she
died during my Panama tour and I wasn't able to return for
her funeral. On my next trip home, I visited her grave with
Mom. Standing over that small plot, I knew I had to make
sure Grandma's tradition of blessing me didn't die with her.

"You will have to bless me when I leave this time," I
said to Mom.

From then on, Mom has never failed to bless me
when we part. Now I could hardly hold back the tears as she
performed the familiar ritual at the Honolulu airport. Then
she and my dad boarded the plane that took them back to
Texas, leaving me with memories I will always treasure.

Recharged and Ready to Fight

The holiday season had provided a much needed break from my struggles with the military. Seeing Lt. Col. Smith's name on the promotion list had been a devastating blow, and I'd desperately needed some time to recover, some time to regain a measure of control over the emotional pain and anguish. There was no doubt in my mind that God had a hand in the sequence of events—the Christmas celebrations and special time with the people I love, and the promotion festivities. Before this break, I'd been lost in an uproar of emotional turmoil and anger. However, the holidays had provided relief from the storm, and as I headed back to work, I felt like my batteries had been recharged. I was ready to take the next step.

Using the address I'd picked up in Japan, I wrote a letter requesting the official results of the CID investigation. On January 5, I faxed it to the Director of the U.S. Army Crime Record Center; Attention: Freedom of Information Office.

For the next week, the first thing I did when I came in to work every morning was look for the return fax. And every morning my stomach would clench anxiously. Somehow I knew I would not be getting good news. The more I thought about what had transpired, the more I questioned the process. When the CID case went to Washington D.C., for review, an Army prosecutor represented me as the complainant. But the prosecution office had never contacted me, and I'd never spoken to the person who represented me. In fact, I didn't even know who he or she was. How had the officer reviewing the case made a decision without talking to me? Most importantly, how did Lt. Col. Smith get selected for promotion to full bird colonel? Shouldn't the system be weeding these guys out? Full colonel was one of the Army's highest honors.

On the morning of January 10, I saw the fax as soon

as I placed my bag on my desk. I remember hesitating
before flipping past the fax transmittal page and taking
several deep breaths. Whatever the news, at least I would
know. I scanned the short, all-in-capital letters paragraph:

STATUS: THIS IS A SUPPLEMENTAL REPORT.
AT 1100, 7 AUG 95, SA 66

COORDINATED WITH CPT XXX WHO
RELATED LTC SMITH HAD RECEIVED A GENERAL
LETTER OF REPRIMAND FOR THE OFFENSES OF
SODOMY, INDECENT ASSAULT, CONDUCT UNBE-
COMING A MEMBER OF THE MILITARY, AND CRU-
ELTY AND MALTREATMENT OF A SUBORDINATE.

How can this be? A general letter of reprimand
(GOLOR) is considered a mere slap on the hand. *What kind
of sick joke is this?* I remembered how Lt. Col. Smith had
said, "If you're thinking of telling anyone, don't be foolish.
No one will believe you." It seemed he'd been right, and I
felt humiliated once again.

Re-reading that paragraph, I began to understand
that the enemy I fought wasn't just Lt. Col. Smith; it was the
entire Army system—a system that could punish the criminal with nothing more than a piece of paper for grave
offenses like sodomy and indecent assault. An obviously
meaningless piece of paper since it didn't even bar his
selection to full colonel.

The next weeks were anguishing ones for me, and
my only comfort from the pain was the time I spent with
Jim. Within the circle of his arms, I felt safe, protected from
the Army. But that didn't mean I wasn't sometimes difficult
and moody, although I tried not to direct my anger towards
him. I grew impatient quickly, my emotions flared erratic-
ally, and sometimes I would cry out loud, "When will I
have peace?" Whenever I went to the office and saw the fax
from CID, I wanted to rush outside and yell loudly to release
the tension I felt. And the sleepless nights were taking their
toll, too, as my nightmares became more intense. Almost
every time I closed my eyes, Lt. Col. Smith would be there,

holding me down. I'd fight off sleep as long as I could, eventually giving in to exhaustion but then waking in terror, kicking of my blankets in an attempt to get *him* off. *When will it end? Where can I turn for help?*

I remembered the conversation I'd had with Col. Driscoll in Washington D.C., about the DACOWITS representative here in Hawaii, a Dr. Young. Nervously I dialed the number. *Please let her be there.*

"Hello," the voice was friendly and full of energy.

"Hello ma'am, is this Dr. Young, the representative for DACOWITS."

"It is."

Whew!

"My name is Major Fischer, and I would like to have an opportunity to meet with you. I was assaulted by my commander about two years ago, and I am very disturbed about the outcome of the case."

Her voice softened, "I'd very much like to meet with you and hear more about your situation. What does your schedule look like on the 16th of January?"

We agreed on a time and place for our meeting, and I hung up the phone feeling encouraged because I knew the Defense Advisory Committee on Women in the Services had had some success in addressing issues concerning women in the military. As soon as I got home that day, I started working on a letter to DACOWITS, so that I could put something in Dr. Young's hand when we met. Writing the letter took several days and was both painful and therapeutic. I began by saying that I was sharing my experiences in the hope that the Army could become a better, safer place for all. Then I highlighted the difficulties I'd had in reporting the case to the proper channels and to the chain of command. I addressed the injustice of the investigative process, describing how the system re-victimized the victim (for example, my psychiatric and hypnotism ordeal), and I shared the disappointment and isolation I'd felt when I discovered fellow soldiers betrayed me.

I also wrote about the difficulty in getting information out of the system, all the way to the ludicrous practice of not informing the victim of his or her case's outcome. And I described my experiences with the medical system, as I sought counseling, and outlined some recommendations of options for rape victims and how sexual harassment complaints might be handled better. I concluded by sharing the disbelief and horror I'd felt when I saw my attacker's name on the recent promotion list and realized the unfortunate message that sent to soldiers and leaders in the Army.

I was clutching this letter in my hand when I climbed the steps of the Pacific Club to meet Dr. Young. *Maintain your composure, Linda. Do not cry, be articulate.* The beautiful, serene setting of one of Honolulu's most prestigious private clubs helped relieve some of the nervousness I felt, and a friendly staff member escorted me immediately to a small waiting room. I had arrived early and while I waited, I reviewed my letter. Dr. Young was right on time. A very impressive Oriental woman in a dark gray suit, she looked the part of a successful executive, and within moments of meeting her, she confirmed that I wouldn't be wasting my time.

"Good afternoon, I'm Dr. Young and you must be Major Fischer," she said warmly, extending her hand. "Please sit down. I've reserved this private room for us."

After we were seated, she said, "I have been looking forward to our meeting, Major Fischer."

"I have, too, Dr. Young, and in preparation, I put this letter together for you, to summarize my experiences over the past few years." I held out the letter.

I sipped ice water anxiously while she read the letter.

Finally she looked up. "With your permission, Major Fischer, I'd like to forward this letter to the main office in Washington D.C." I nodded my assent, and she placed the letter in her briefcase. "I want you to know I recognize the courage it takes to come forward, Major Fischer," she said, "And I promise I will assist in any way that I can."

During the next few hours, I told Dr. Young my story in more detail. Although I tried not to cry, I did break into tears once or twice, because talking about the assault was still very difficult for me. Then we discussed each of the issues I'd raised in my letter. At the close of our meeting, she expressed concern that I was not in a counseling program.

"I have a friend who provides counseling services with the Veteran's Administration Center. Would you be interested in meeting with her?" she asked. "I'd be happy to set up the appointment and go with you to meet her."

When I agreed, Dr. Young phoned her friend directly from the small meeting room. By the time she hung up, I had an 8:00 a.m. appointment to see a counselor at the VA Center in about a week.

"Dr. Young, thank you for taking time from your busy schedule to meet with me and for your genuine concern," I said.

"Well, I can't promise you anything, but I'm going to send this letter to the main office. You and I will meet again next week at the counselor's office." She gave me a quick hug.

Walking to my car in the tree-shaded parking lot after we parted, I smiled to myself. Taking action felt good.

On the day of my counseling appointment, the sun rose bright and clear, I felt a little more anxious than usual as I dressed in jeans and a T-shirt. Because of my experiences, I was still hesitant to be involved with a government counseling program, and I couldn't easily shake the fear that any record of counseling might have an adverse affect on what was left of my career. But I swallowed my nervousness and headed downtown.

A cheerful Dr. Young met me as we had agreed, and introduced me to the counselor, a Dr. Karen Layton. She took the time to explain my situation as I had told it to her. By the time she excused herself, she had confirmed the favorable impression I'd picked up at our last meeting. I felt she went way beyond the call of duty! Her presence had eased my anxiety, and I felt somewhat more comfortable when Dr. Layton, a motherly-looking woman with metal "granny-glasses", began the session. After I'd filled out some paperwork, she explained that I was eligible for limited counseling (six visits) at the VA facility and that she would maintain my counseling record at the VA office.

For the rest of our session, we talked about what had happened to me, but despite Dr. Layton's pleasant personality and professional demeanor, I had difficulty opening up. I'd bottled up so much turmoil inside me for too long, and old habits die hard. We did, however, set a date for my next appointment before I left. Although I knew I had left much unsaid, I felt a sense of relief. At least now I had an outlet. And I hadn't felt any stigma connected with my visit. I was relieved the office wasn't on a military base, I could feel comfortable and relaxed. Best of all, I had a sense that my confidentiality would be honored and the information I gave wasn't going to be hung out on a line for the whole Army to see.

Although I was relieved that I'd found an opportunity for counseling, it still troubled me that I'd had to hear about it through Dr. Young rather than the Army medical system. I called the Army Medical Center's hospital commander. When I learned there had been a recent change of command and the new commander hadn't arrived yet, I made an appointment to meet with the deputy commander. I hoped I could at least ensure that from now on, women who called the Army needing help would get better information.

The next weekend was Super Bowl Sunday, and I made sure I was free to spend the day with Jim. This meant fighting to keep my calendar clear. I'd begun officiating every weekend and many week nights, and whenever I had spare time, I'd get requests to do more games. I knew that officiating helped me with my explosive behavior—I had to keep my cool on the court. And it certainly got me out of the house and gave me less time to fret about the events of the last two years. But no way would I work on Super Bowl Sunday! Being with Jim, my calm in the storm, was far more important.

The week after the Super Bowl passed quickly, and soon it was time for my appointment at the Medical Center. As I drove up the hill to the massive pink hospital, I could feel a sense of purpose heating up inside me. I was on a mission. *No one else should have to go through what I have.*

Sitting across from the deputy commander, however, I was careful to maintain a cool demeanor, because I knew it wouldn't help if my anger showed through. I explained my situation and described my experiences with the Army when I had inquired about a counseling program. He listened intently and pledged to raise the issues I'd raised. And then our short meeting was over. Since that day, I've wondered what the current response would be to a victim who wanted counseling services elsewhere, but I've never picked up the phone. I suppose I just don't want to be disappointed.

In early February, I received a response from the executive director of DACOWITS. She informed me that her committee couldn't address individual issues or concerns, but that she would forward my letter to the Assistant Secretary of Army for Manpower and Reserve Affairs.

I'm not sure what I had expected. I did know that what I read sounded like a form letter, and I couldn't help but feel lost in the shuffle, unsure of what the next step should be. I *was* sure, however, that I wasn't satisfied yet. Too many questions had been left unanswered. When I'd figured out what the next step should be, I'd take it!

End of the Line

It didn't take me long to decide that my next step should be to write to the Inspector General of the Army. One of my responsibilities with the Corps of Engineers is to perform duties as the Acting Inspector General for this division, and those duties include functioning as a kind of ombudsman, listening to employee complaints and problem solving with them. So I thought maybe the Army Inspector General could do the same for me. I wrote a long letter—including everything I'd included in my letter to DACOWITS and more—and was preparing to fax it to Washington D.C., when I received an invitation to attend a luncheon featuring none other than *the* Inspector General of the Army. He would be in Hawaii speaking to a large group of us. *Talk about divine intervention! This is my opportunity!*

The day of the luncheon, I had butterflies in my stomach. *What will I say if I actually have the chance to speak to him?* I wasn't only nervous about speaking to him; I also felt uncomfortable having to socialize with other soldiers in the military. Before the assault, I'd played, exercised, and traveled with my Army buddies. Now I avoided contact whenever possible.

When I arrived at the luncheon, which was held in an officers' club, I chose a table near a door so I could make my escape if necessary. My tablemates, none of whom I knew, and I made polite introductions and then equally polite conversation during the buffet until General Randolph stepped to the podium. *At first I listened carefully to his remarks, but then my attention wandered as I thought about those last days in Panama and what had followed. I could feel my face flush and my eyes moisten. I took a couple of deep breaths, fighting to focus on his remarks.* Soon the general concluded his speech to the audience's applause.

While soldiers milled around—some making their way to shake the general's hand, others departing—I stood in a corner of the room watching. Then, when the line in front of the general shortened, I went over and joined in. Soon I was standing in front of the tall, distinguished-looking officer. I reached for his hand.

"Sir, my name is Major Linda Fischer. I am the Acting IG for the Pacific Ocean Division Corps of Engineers."

"It's good to meet you."

"Sir, almost two years ago now, I was assaulted by my battalion commander." I heard the tremor in my voice, but I kept going. "I was a company commander at the time. The whole experience has been brutal, the assault, the investigation, and now his recent selection for promotion to colonel. This morning I faxed a letter to your office, detailing my experiences over the last couple of years, so I just wanted you to see the face that goes along with the letter. Thank you for your time."

I began to move on, but the general stopped me and asked me for my name and number. Fortunately, I could give him a business card that I'd stuck in the small notepad I carried—just in case. Then I walked in a daze to my car. *I can't believe I got to talk to him! And I didn't cry! Now when he reads my letter—and I'll bet he reads hundreds of letters—he'll have a face to put to a name.* Faces were the human element that seemed to be missing from the military system.

Now all I could do was wait. That night I went for a run just before sunset, pounding the pavement while the last rays of light disappeared into the darkness and city lights sprang up around me. Then I went reluctantly to bed, wondering if my nights would ever be free from haunting nightmares, if I would ever find peace. Unfortunately, I had another restless night. When I dragged myself out of bed the next morning, I could recall seeing my bedside clock read 3 a.m., 4:32 a.m., and 5:16 a.m. By the time I arrived at work, the first thing I wanted was a shot of caffeine. I'd take care of the yellow slip on my desk asking me to call the IG's office right away as soon as I had a mug of coffee in my hand.

Maria met me at the coffee pot. "Hey, good morning. I made the coffee weak the way you like it. Did you call the IG office?"

"No, I'll get to it soon." I spooned sugar and powdered cream into my coffee. "Did they say what it was about?"

"They said something about a meeting with the general."

Hot coffee spilled over my hand as I spun around and headed for my office. Once there I dialed the number on the yellow slip and hung up a few minutes later with an appointment for later that day. I would be meeting face to face with the Inspector General of the Army at Schofield Barracks. This was more than unbelievable! Part of me was elated, the other part nervous during the rest of the day—a long day that dragged painfully on, minute by minute—until finally it was time to leave for Schofield. I took with me a copy of the letter I had faxed to the IG's D.C. office.

When I sat down at a conference table across from General Randolph, I had no idea what to expect. But I knew I'd been granted a rare opportunity. *Another chance to tell your story to someone who can make a difference, who can make things better, Linda.* A few papers rested on the table in front of the general, and I recognized the one on the top immediately. It was my officer record brief, which is a kind of one-page snapshot of your career. *They probably know more about us than we do.*

I handed him a copy of the letter I had faxed to his office in Washington D.C., but he asked me to share my experience and thoughts with me before he read it. I hardly knew where to start, but I couldn't let this opportunity pass. I took a deep breath and told my story one more time, ending with the words, "Sir, I will tell you that it has been a harsh and humiliating experience, one I would not wish on my worst enemy."

The general looked thoughtful. "Major Fischer, the investigation is over and punishment was administered. He received a letter of reprimand. I don't think anything can be done to change that now, so what is it that I can do for you?"

Fortunately I'd made a short bullet outline of issues and concerns from the letter, I started with the first one and worked my way down. I talked about all the problems inherent in the system that I'd mentioned in my DACOWITS letter, and I added a few others. For example, the fact that although the Staff Judge Advocate here in Hawaii had made my case file available to my current commander, they wouldn't tell *me* anything.

"In most of my interactions with the system since I reported the assault, I haven't felt that anyone was protecting *my* rights," I explained. "The system seems to provide a lot more support for the accused than for the victim."

While the general listened intently and took notes, I suggested a number of recommendations for improving the situation. The Army should have a strict process for documenting complaints and passing on that information, I told the general. A case in point: during the CID investigation of my case, a soldier had told the investigator that Lt. Col. Smith had received a previous complaint of sexual harassment. However, the details couldn't be verified because they weren't passed up the chain of command and recorded, so they were considered "hearsay" and had to be left out of the final report. Too often, particularly when the offender is a promising "high-speed guy", a complaint is swept under the carpet.

"In my opinion, all complaints need to be well-documented and passed up to the post-level EO office, and a commander who engages in covering up complaints or leaving this information off of performance reports should be held accountable," I said. "Otherwise, when a commander fails to act, the offender moves on to his next assignment and the cycle continues."

I also talked about the need for appropriate counseling options—and, if necessary, separation options—for military women who are assaulted or raped.

"It's my hope, sir, that my concerns could be useful in developing, implementing, and improving policies and programs in the Army which are designed to eliminate sexual harassment and support the victims of today and tomorrow."

The general and I talked for over an hour, and when I left, I felt that he really wanted to make a difference, to improve the situation for women in the military. That feeling was priceless.

Several weeks later, the Army IG office wrote to tell me that they would be conducting an inquiry into my experiences with the various Army systems and processes. I'd be contacted in the near future for a telephone interview.

That interview took place on March 14, after I'd provided them with a requested chronology of events—dates, places, names of people in Panama and Texas during the time of the assault and the investigation. When I picked up the phone to talk to a Lieutenant Colonel Braxton, I had no idea we would be on the phone for over two hours.

Lt. Col. Braxton began by informing me that our conversation would be recorded. Then he administered a long-distance oath. I raised my right hand while he intoned, "Do you swear that the testimony you are about to give shall be the truth, the whole truth, and nothing but the truth, so help you God?"

"I do."

"The purpose of this interview is to review your request for DAIG assistance as presented in your 7 February 1996 letter to General Randolph. The expectation is we will be able to conclude this interview with a clear idea of what you expect. To do this, we will review various portions of your letter in order to clarify your concerns and to make it possible for us to determine which matters are appropriate for an IG to resolve. Therefore, we'll be asking numerous questions with the sole purpose of eliminating confusion and of clarifying your concerns."

Together we went through the entire chronology from April of 1991 to the present—who, where, what, when. Then we reviewed my listing of contacts between Smith and me since I'd left Panama—the card he'd sent to my parents house, my first report of the incident to my commander at Lackland AFB, and the letter from my attorney to him.

"What was the purpose of that letter, Major Fischer?"

"The purpose was to let Lieutenant Colonel Smith know that I wanted no further contact from him written, verbal, physical, or through a third party."

"And you apparently know when that letter was received?"

"Right. I have a copy of the certified receipt from the United States Postal Service and it shows his signature on it and it's dated … 24 December is the date that it's stamped that he signed it and 26 December is the date that it's signed for return."

As I answered questions on the reporting and investigation process, the betrayal of peers and officers, and the counseling issue, I could feel the frustration again, the hurt, as if I were being pulled once more into a black hole. My voice began to crack with emotion when I told Lt. Col. Braxton about the frustration of trying to find counseling.

He must have sensed that I was nearing the breaking point. "Okay, I'm going off record," he said.

Knowing that I was no longer being recorded allowed me to release my tears. "You feel like you're in a fishbowl and that you have a label on your forehead that says 'I reported a rape,'" I said, weeping. "And then, if you want to get counseling, they want you to go to a medical facility and see a military doctor. So you just feel like more attention is focused on you."

Lt. Col. Braxton responded sympathetically, and soon we were able to resume the formal interview. After I'd answered a few more questions, he said, "I'd like to conclude this interview by asking—what is it that you expect from the DAIG?"

I told Lt. Col. Braxton what I had told General Randolph. "I'm hoping that sharing my experiences will help to make changes to a system that should be more flexible in supporting victims. That when we identify victims, they'll get information right away about what kinds of help is available to them so that they're not left just kind of hanging in a gray area. That the victim can go and get counseling in an environment where she can feel relaxed and safe. That there will be changes in Equal Opportunity reporting procedures of sexual harassment or assault of that type. That post-level records be kept about complaints and offenses and that commanders be held accountable for acting on complaints. That when an officer or noncommissioned officer does receive a letter of reprimand, that letter would affect his or her performance rating."

We concluded with Lt. Col. Braxton's request that I not discuss our conversation with anyone but an attorney, as long as these matters were under investigation, and I agreed. However, when he asked if I would consent to the release of my testimony outside official channels, I said "no." I didn't feel confident that my testimony wouldn't somehow be used against me. Then Lt. Col. Braxton signed off, leaving me slumped at my desk, emotionally drained.

Before I heard back from the IG, I received another piece of dispiriting news. For the last several years, as part of a downsizing effort, the Army had been offering a fifteen year retirement option. I was nearing fourteen years and had planned to take advantage of the option. Although my benefits would be decreased, I felt I could hang on another year and then leave with at least some dignity. Then the bad news came. Because the fifteen year option had worked so well and the ranks of officers had been thinned effectively, the Army was canceling the early retirement plan next year—right before I made my fifteen years. I'd have to resign now and forfeit my benefits or stay in for six more years. *Six years! How could I survive that long?* Meanwhile, I'd heard through the grapevine that Lt. Col. Smith was retiring soon with all his benefits, of course. *Something is terribly wrong with this picture!*

It was June before a letter arrived from the Office of the Inspector General. I remember sitting in my office chair for a long time, looking at the unopened envelope on my desk and rocking back and forth. I didn't want to open that letter! Sometimes you feel like you just can't take another disappointment.

I should have left it unopened. The letter began, "A thorough inquiry was conducted into the matters you presented. The Inspector General (TIG) personally reviewed your allegations and issues and the results of our inquiry to ensure that all of the concerns were appropriately addressed. Each allegation or issue is discussed below." It went on to dismiss *all* my concerns except for one: the fact that the Fort Sam Houston CID agents did not properly advise me of my rights to contact the Victim Liaison Representative. The letter did say that "as a result of the concerns you presented regarding the Army's lack of appropriate sensitivity to the assistance needs of victims of sexual assault, TIG has tasked the Medical Command (MEDCOM) IG to closely examine and to formally report on the adequacy of policies and procedures currently in place at our mental health facilities."

I flipped the pages over, as if I would find something more on the back. *This is it? This is the response? I sent them a seven-page letter, gave a two-hour interview, and they respond with a two-page memo? What about my EO concerns? What about holding commanders responsible for not taking action? What about making annotations of offenses mandatory on performance reports?*

I was outraged enough to call the IG office in D.C. and track down the colonel who had signed the letter. Considering my mood, he was graciously polite and promised to have an IG representative call me back the next day with some answers.

"Major Fischer, all those other issues you raised aren't considered IG concerns, so we couldn't address them on our response," a pleasant female voice told me the next day.

"Then you should say that in your response! Otherwise, the person who gets the letter feels really unheard and frustrated," I explained. "So, whose concerns *are* those issues the IG office can't address?"

The representative hesitated. "I don't know." I could tell she shared some of my frustration, that she knew as well as I did that the system had some serious holes.

"So what am I supposed to do next?" I asked.

"We sent your memo on to Medical Command and asked them to formally report back. Let's wait to see how they respond."

And that was that. I had exhausted all military channels for restitution or changes, and the thought that I was locked in the Army with no way out except resignation disheartened me. The flicker of light at the end of tunnel had dimmed until I sensed the slightest breeze could extinguish it. How would I pass through the tunnel—another six years in the Army? Although I felt relatively safe with the Corps of Engineers, my tour with them would end in a year, and then the Army could move me.

Out my window I could see the MP building across the street, and I knew I could never be a part of that world again. The Army, an organization I once served so proudly, had become my enemy.

Time for Healing

It was a dark time in my life. I felt like I was in a spinning black hole, nothing to hold on to, no way to pull myself out.

One night I left my apartment for a walk, as I did so many evenings now. I trudged along in the darkness, dragging my feet on the pavement and hardly bothering to wipe the tears from my eyes. A hollow, empty sensation threatened to overwhelm me. *I can't take any more.*

Suddenly tires screeched, a horn blasted, bright lights blinded me, and I felt a rush of air, the force of a car passing only inches from me. I stumbled back toward the sidewalk where I clutched a light pole on the corner to steady myself. *You just walked out in front of a car, Linda!* I was horrified. For all my despondency, I didn't want to give up *life!*

After I got my bearings—I was down by the zoo about a mile from my apartment— I started home. But in that moment, something changed for me. I realized I'd reached the point at which I *had* to make changes if I was to recover from the assault and its draining aftermath. It was time for healing.

Counseling would be one route, but it was slow going. Although I was making some progress at the VA Center's counseling program, I suspect it was like pulling teeth for Dr. Layton. She had to pull every piece of information from deep inside me, from that same black hole that threatened to engulf me because, although I yearned to be free of that night, that year, I just didn't want to talk about it one more time. I'm sure it took Dr. Layton the first six sessions just to pry the story from me. What I didn't know at the time was that she was going the extra mile for me. Aware of my aversion to the Army Medical Center, she had requested and received an exception to policy so that I could continue in the VA program after the initial sessions. When I

learned what she had done, I let her know how much I
appreciated her concern. Still I needed more.

I remembered Jim telling me about a personal
improvement program he'd completed some years earlier.
Whenever he talked about a problem or something going on,
he would refer to this program, and I could see its positive
impact on his life. *Maybe I'll try that.* I searched all over the
house for the piece of paper on which I'd written the name
of the program. Sure I could have just picked up the phone
and called Jim, but I felt like I had to do this on my own.
Ah, here was the guy's name. Anthony Robbins. I went to a
bookstore and found a book Anthony Robbins had written.
The back of the book gave me a phone number, and I
hurried home to place the call.

"I want the 30-day program," I said.

The voice on the other end of the line tried to swing
into what I suppose was his usual sales pitch.

"No, no, you already have a sale. Do you take credit
cards?"

Once I'd made up my mind, I was ready to jump in,
although at the time I had no idea what a tremendous impact
Anthony Robbins' 30 Day Personal Power Program would
have on my life.

When the set of audio tapes arrived, I listened on
my way to work, on my way to ball games, and at home.
I immersed myself in the tapes, sometimes listening to the
same one two days in a row, to be sure I didn't miss anything. This meant taking more than thirty days to finish the
program, but I wanted to really absorb what I was hearing
and to thoroughly complete each daily exercise.

Before I was halfway through, Jim began to notice
positive differences in my behavior and attitude. So did my
co-workers who told me that I seemed excited about life,
that I smiled more often. I know my energy level soared. By
the time I completed the program, I had set personal and
monetary goals and had begun to understand some of the
obstacles I'd been allowing to stand in my way.

Just the act of setting goals allowed me to get some
long-time projects off the ground. One of the exercises asks

you to make a list of things you want to do but have been
putting off. Then you take care of one item on your list
every day.

Writing a book about my experience with the Army
was one item on my list. I'd thought about it for months and
even talked to a friend in Texas about it. He'd given me the
number of a woman who might help me, but I'd been
waiting for...for I wasn't sure what. Now I pulled the
number from a pile of paperwork on my desk and made the
call, and within a week this book saw its beginning. I still
didn't know much about what I was doing, but what was
exciting—and energizing—was that I'd taken the first step.

Another project that became a reality was producing
and marketing bookmarks. For years I'd loved my Grandma
Stephens' inspirational poems, especially one called "If
Jesus Had A Telephone," and I'd always thought they would
make nice bookmarks. Now I typed them into the computer
and used my graphics program to format them into book-
mark size. Then I met with the representative of a local
printing plant, and within a month, I'd placed my first order.
My Grandma Stephens is a very special lady, and it's hard to
describe the gratification I felt inside the first time I showed
her one of "her" bookmarks. Since that first printing, I've
sold hundreds of the bookmarks, and we've both benefited
financially and in other ways, too.

The next project arose from an everyday need.
I officiate at a lot of games—football, basketball, and
softball—almost every night of the week, and no matter
what sport I'm working, I have to wear highly shined black
athletic shoes. Because the polishes I'd tried didn't seem to
last long, I had to shine my shoes every day, and there's
nothing very exciting about shining shoes! Several months
before I listened to the Anthony Robbins' tapes, I'd decided
there had to be a better way, so I'd played around in the
kitchen with different waxes and colors until I came up with
a homemade polish that lasted three or four days. Although I
thought the final result was good enough to sell, I made just
enough to use on my own athletic shoes and boots. The
Robbins' tapes got me moving.

I sent off to the mainland for some bottles and bottle caps with daubers to apply the polish and before I knew it, I was in business. Now I bottle the stuff—Proshine, I call it—make the labels on my computer, and sell it out of the trunk of my car, usually to the referees and umpires I work with.

With the bookmarks and the shoe polish in production, I decided to give my ventures a name. "Unlimited Incorporated", I call myself. Can you imagine? All this productivity just from listening to a set of tapes.

Since my introduction to Anthony Robbins' philosophy, I've been going non-stop. I can't say I don't have bad days. I do, and I never forget how easily I could slip into the black hole again, but I find I recover more quickly now. What the 30-day program did was give me new tools to carry in my toolbox, and they are there when I need them.

One of the most important benefits of the program was the desire it instilled in me for more—more of the same thing, more motivational books and programs. Now a stack of books sit in my living room, and when I finish one I start the next. When someone mentions a book they've read, I ask lots of questions. What's it about? What makes it good? Then I check it out. One of the first books I read was *Tongue Fu: How to Deflect, Disarm, and Defuse Any Verbal Conflict* by Sam Horn. Considering my volatile state, this book was a valuable tool to add to my toolbox. I found the book's suggestions helpful for me in my work environment where I was especially sensitive to everything said about women in the military. And I found it useful with my officiating duties, too.

Understanding more about how the mind works was another benefit I garnered from the Robbins program. I learned that if you connect a negative association with some experience or activity, you'll avoid it as much as possible. So to make a change, you have to develop a positive association with that experience. An example for me was participating in sports. All my life, I'd been an avid sportswoman, and when I first met Lt. Col. Smith, I'd enjoyed running, biking, fishing and racquetball with him. Then, as I began to dread our time together, I developed an aversion to these activities. At first I found refuge on the golf course, but eventually I avoided taking part in any sport, even the running that had been an important part of my life since junior high.

In San Antonio, I literally could not run. Less than a half mile down the road, I'd start wheezing and gasping. I couldn't breathe. Just like I couldn't breathe when Lt. Col. Smith's body was crushing the air from my lungs. I'll never know how long my running associations would have remained negative if Millie hadn't arrived in San Antonio with her team. That was the positive association I needed, and now running is a pleasurable experience for me again—as is biking. I still avoid racquetball and fishing, but I know that in time, the right moment will present itself, and I'll break those barriers, too.

Late that summer, I experienced a moving example of overcoming a negative association, at least for a brief moment. The Knight family had stopped on their way from Okinawa to the mainland, and we were packing as much fun into a few days as we could when Julie invited me to join their family at a barbecue in Mililani. Our hosts would be some long-time friends of the Knights, Richard and Martha Reed. Julie had warned me that Richard had cancer and didn't have long to live.

"If you feel uncomfortable joining us, I'll understand," she said.

I didn't want to miss a moment with one of my favorite families, however, so I headed out to the town where I had lived so many years earlier. At the Reed home, Julie introduced me to Richard, a former Navy Seal now so ravaged with cancer he needed a wheel chair, his wife Martha, and Richard's parents, who had come to the Islands to be with their terminally-ill son.

For the next few hours, over barbecued chicken and potato salad at a little community park, I got to know this brave family. When I listened to Richard's parents tell stories about their son, my heart went out to them. And when Richard and I spent some talking about his military career, I was all ears. Navy Seals do some pretty amazing things! Never having been close to anyone with cancer before, I was impressed with the energy he still displayed. He was determined to enjoy all that today had to offer and then to live another day. I shared with him how much I missed holding a command and working with my troops. It wasn't until dark that I headed back to my apartment, thinking what a great time I'd had, but not expecting to hear from the Reeds again.

So I was surprised to get a call from Martha Reed several weeks later. She told me that her husband had passed away and invited me to the funeral which would be at sea.

I offered her my condolences and then, because I hadn't been to a funeral since I was a child, I asked her what the appropriate attire would be. Aloha attire, she said, which in Hawaii means casual wear. After I hung up, I was checking my closet to see what I could wear when the phone rang again.

"Linda, could you wear your uniform? It would mean a lot to Richard's mother and father. They were very impressed by you at the picnic. And you really touched Richard that day. Especially when you called him 'sir.' He felt you accorded him a dignity and respect he'd lost when he had to leave the service." She hesitated. "So could...could you wear your uniform?"

The only answer was "Yes, of course."

I pulled my green dress uniform from the closet and hung it on the door. As I gazed at it, tears ran down my face. I only wore an Army uniform when I absolutely had to. But for Richard and his family, I'd make an exception. Before the funeral, I spent some time on that uniform, checking the awards and polishing the brass. I starched my shirt and pressed military creases into it. I polished my shoes and brushed my hat. Then, pulling a cardboard box down from the top of my closet, I retrieved my white gloves, sheathed in clear protective plastic.

When I arrived at the dock where Richard's family was gathered, I was dressed as sharply as a soldier going for a board or special ceremony. We embarked, and while the boat took us out to sea, Richard's bereaved parents and wife told stories about him. They were obviously grieving, but also experiencing relief that he would suffer no more. All I wanted was to be a source of strength for Richard's family and to honor the memory of his service to our country. For the first time in two years, I felt proud to wear my uniform. A positive association.

I can't say that the experience at Richard's funeral permanently changed my bad feelings about wearing an Army uniform. I still wait until the last moment before I leave in the morning to put mine on, and I take it off the minute I walk in the door after work. But I did learn that I can temporarily overcome a negative association under certain circumstances.

All in all, the Anthony Robbins program has helped me to make tremendous changes in my life. Some victories have been greater than others, but all—no matter how small—matter. It gave me the resolve to work at changing what I could in the time I had left in the Army.

The Army's Reputation Under Fire

November 7th, 1996. I was sitting on the sofa, eating a bowl of cereal and not really paying much attention to the morning news on television. What was this? Something about soldiers being charged with sexual misconduct at the Aberdeen Proving Ground in Maryland? Trainees accusing drill sergeants of rape and harassment? I grabbed the remote and turned up the volume.

For the next half hour I sat stunned while I watched the breaking of a story that came to be known as the Aberdeen scandals. The young soldiers standing before the microphones on national TV would send a shock wave throughout the nation and bring attention to a serious problem in the military. Ironically, it was an internal Army investigation that triggered the story and the eventual charging of two sergeants and a captain with raping and sexually harassing at least 17 female soldiers at the Aberdeen installation.

It was hard to leave for work that morning. I didn't want to miss a moment of the unfolding story. *You can watch at work, Linda.* I made good time on the freeway, and as soon as I got to the office, I turned on the TV. No cable, no CNN news! I had to wait until I returned home that evening.

That evening, watching the recap from the morning's release, I felt angered as I listened to female recruits tell of being manipulated and assaulted by their drill sergeants. Their story was in part my story. And I felt sadness, too. It's never been a secret that sexual harassment occurs in the military, at least not for us inside the system. But for seasoned Army soldiers, commissioned and non-commissioned alike, to commit such bold and heinous acts was incomprehensible. The Army faced embarrassment and a barrage of criticism from all sides, and our nation watched closely to see what the official reaction would be.

The accused soldiers (and their number grew to over a dozen within a few short weeks) were immediately relieved of duty, and the Army began the process of interviewing every female trainee who had been at the Aberdeen school in the last two years. The Army also installed a sexual harassment hotline, to which nearly 1,700 calls came within three days of the Aberdeen news release. Many of these were from people expressing an opinion, but about 100 were from callers making new complaints. In just four months, the hot line would receive over 4,000 calls, and before it was closed, it would log over 7,500 calls, approximately 1,000 of which included serious allegations that criminal investigators pursued.

The weeks following Aberdeen were difficult ones for me. Reading the articles and editorials, watching the frequent TV specials—Dateline, 20/20, 48 Hours—reopened old wounds and triggered painful memories. I deeply admired the young women who had come forward, for I knew it had taken a great deal of courage to tell their stories. I knew, too, the difficulties they had encountered and the ones that still lay ahead. I felt their pain and hoped that some day they would find peace. And I hoped that the Army leadership would view Aberdeen as an opportunity to make significant improvements to current policies and procedures that would better the lot of women in the military.

Aberdeen seemed to open the floodgates. On November 12, a similar case of drill sergeants having sex with recruits surfaced at Fort Leonard Wood. On November 25, the public heard about an earlier incident at Fort Sam Houston. In February, 1997, in Darmstadt, Germany, allegations were made that three instructors had sexually assaulted or harassed 11 women soldiers.

For several months, I could hardly pick up a paper or turn on the TV without reading about sexual assault and harassment in the military. The media raised the questions that so badly needed answering. Just how prevalent was the abuse of power in the Army? Did superiors frequently intimidate and coerce soldiers? And what about reporting procedures? What happened when a woman reported abuse?

Was she protected from retaliation? How effective was the chain of command in handling cases? Although I didn't know how the Army would respond, I found a certain satisfaction in seeing national newspapers raise so many of the questions I'd asked for several years, and I hoped the leadership would listen more closely to the voice of the media than it had to me.

About this time, the Pentagon released the results of a survey confirming the problem of sexual harassment in all armed forces branches, with a finger pointed most critically at the Army and Marine Corps. The Army Times headlined its November 1996 story, "Harassment Highest in Army Corps."

The survey results were damning: "The Army and the Marine Corps led all the services in 1995 in the frequency of reported instances of sexual harassment...nearly one in 10 women in the Army and Marine Corps had been sexually assaulted within the past year...nearly two in 10 were the targets of 'sexual coercion'...Army women have lost some faith in their senior leadership's efforts to combat the problem... fewer than half of Army women believed the service's senior leadership, or the senior leadership of their installation, has been making 'honest and reasonable efforts' to stop sexual harassment."

Reading that the survey showed "sexual harassment in the military appears to have dropped in recent years" didn't cheer me up much. Not when the Army's numbers had declined a mere 7% from 68% of women reporting sexual harassment in 1988 to 61% in 1995. It brought into question the coined phrase: "zero tolerance." Would any corporation in the world tolerate such high numbers?

Under the watchful eye of Congress, the Army formed two working groups: the Senior Review Panel on Sexual Harassment and the Inspector General Task Force, which investigated Initial Entry Training. The January 1997 issue of Army Magazine said, "Secretary West chartered the Senior Review Panel on Sexual Harassment to 'recommend those changes necessary to improve the human relations environment in which soldiers live and work, with the specific goal of eradicating sexual harassment in the Army,' according to officials." The panel would gather information for more than six months, visiting 59 military installations worldwide and surveying 30,000 troops.

One of the soldiers selected to serve on the Senior Review Panel was Command Sergeant Major Gene McKinney, the top ranking non-commissioned officer in the Army. At the time of his appointment to the panel, I didn't realize that the whole nation would be hearing a lot more about him in the very near future. But I did have hopes that Army leadership would finally begin to address the issues I'd been struggling with for three long years.

Doing Time

Late in the fall, 1996, news of the pervasive sexual harassment in the military continued to make national headlines. I began to believe that telling my story could somehow make a difference—not only for women in the military but for all women in male-dominated workplaces. I decided to contact a local congresswoman and present my concerns to her.

On the day of our appointment, the Hawaiian skies were their usual brilliant blue, even though it was December. A few white clouds, chased by trade winds, headed out to sea, and I let the breeze cool me for a moment before I entered the Federal Building. I had prepared carefully for this meeting; a notebook that included information gathered from surveys plus clippings of recent articles from the paper as well as a record of my own experiences was tucked under my arm. But I was still nervous about meeting with a woman who had spent so much of her life in the halls of Congress. Could my actions *really* make a difference? *At least you are doing something, Linda.*

A few moments with Hawaii's warm and caring representative put me at ease. Her years of wisdom and knowledge were evident, and we plunged right into conversation. I told her much of what I had told the IG and the DACOWITS representatives, emphasizing the need for speedier, consistent action from Army leaders and better victim protection.

"The Army's definition of sexual harassment is clear, and soldiers *do* know what is acceptable and unacceptable," I said. "The problem is with the action—or lack of action, actually—on the part of the commanders. They tend to take action based on what they've seen as they've moved up in the military and very often sweep the whole mess under the carpet, just moving people around. They look the other way, even in cases of repeat offenders, and send the message that sexual harassment is okay."

From the representative's responses, I learned that Congress shared many of my concerns, especially since Aberdeen, and was looking for answers from the different branches of the Armed Services. However, the issue of appropriate counseling and other provisions for victims didn't seem to have caught Congress' attention quite so strongly, and the congresswoman wanted to hear more.

"No soldier wants to be seen going to the mental ward," I explained. "Sexual assault and harassment victims need to get counseling in an environment outside the military, with the military picking up the cost."

I also talked about the difficulties victims of sexual harassment face when they want to leave the military early. "Bringing a charge and going through a lengthy investigation is a painful and humiliating experience. Many women choose to leave quietly, even though they may lose their benefits, just to escape the further humiliation of being labeled with psychiatric disorders under the military system. This isn't right. If what's happened to them has left them unable to function in the military, they should be given an administrative discharge and compensated for their losses, based on the number of years they have served."

During our conversation about this issue, I sensed there might be major political finger pointing going on in D.C. The Army was saying its hands were tied because Congress did not allow for such provisions, and Congress was asking, "What are *you* going to do about this issue?"

At the end of our spirited conversation, the congresswoman asked me to come back when I'd heard from the Army Medical Command on the topic of counseling provisions for women. This was the one issue from my long memo to the IG's office that had not yet been responded to. With what felt like an eternity to serve in the Army, I had time. I'd be back.

The next day I left for Texas to celebrate Christmas early with my family. Then I returned, and Jim and I shared Christmas and New Year's in Hawaii. As I turned my calendar to 1997, I reflected that 1996 had been a year of ups and downs, highs and lows. I'd learned that Lt. Col.

Smith had received only a slap on the wrist for his actions and that he had been allowed to retire with full benefits. I'd been disappointed by the memos from the IG's office and from DACOWTS, and I'd missed the fifteen year retirement cutoff. But with my back against the wall, I'd fought back, and thanks to the Anthony Robbins' tapes, I'd made some new beginnings. Now I had some small hope that perhaps the Army, its reputation under fire, might be ready to make some changes, too. Perhaps 1997 would be a better year for both the Army and for Maj. Linda A. Fischer.

Ever since I'd talked to the Inspector General's D.C. office in June, I'd been calling the representative there to find out the status of the response from Medical Command. I had the letter from the local hospital denying counseling outside the psychiatric ward at the medical center, so now all I could do was wait to see what the Department of the Army had to say. With all the specials on TV and articles in the paper echoing the need for better assistance to soldiers who experienced sexual assault and harassment, surely the Army would take a closer look at its policies. Obviously, no one could claim any more that women in the military were happy with the status quo!

Unfortunately, when the IG representative called me early in the new year, I knew immediately from her tone that her news would not be encouraging. "Medical Command states that current provisions for counseling are adequate."

"You're kidding!" I said, although I knew she wasn't. When I asked for a copy of the memo that gave this opinion, I was once again "stonewalled" and she told me I'd have to request it through the Freedom of Information Act. *Been there, done that!* However, unlike the local victim liaison officer I'd spoken to some months earlier, at least she gave me the information I needed.

"But it could take some time to get your request filled," she warned. "They are really backlogged." Which turned out to be an understatement as I made the request right after our phone call and didn't get an answer until September, nine months later.

In the meantime, a new concern was rearing its ugly head. During the past eighteen months, I'd become more comfortable with my job with the Corps of Engineers. Working predominantly with civilians allowed me to feel like I was no longer in the Army, and I avoided all contact with the Military Police, never crossing the street, and turning down invitations to all MP functions—whether conferences, meetings, training, or social events. Now, with my Corps of Engineers tour running out, my anxiety level began to rise.

I can't go back into the MP world!

Dr. Layton, my counselor at the VA center, grew concerned about the turmoil I was going through. "How much longer can you take this, Linda?" she would ask.

"As long as it takes to find a way to leave with dignity and respect," I said. "I will not resign." Brave talk, but I knew that the IG had checked with PERSCOM, the controller of all personnel administrative actions and that there were no provisions for me to get out without requesting a medical discharge. I knew, too, that I couldn't go back into the Army environment. Being around MPs again might destroy me emotionally. I hated the thought of facing a medical board, just another military system as far as I was concerned, and I hated the thought of the psychological labeling that might result, but I reluctantly agreed to Dr. Layton's request to inquire about the process on my behalf.

At the same time, I looked for another option, talking with Col. Wilcott about applying for what we call an In Place Consecutive Overseas Tour (IPCOT). If I were granted an IPCOT, I would be able to stay with the Corps of Engineers several more years, almost until retirement. Since it looked like I had to do my time, my choice would be to stay in my present environment where I could continue counseling and avoid most MP contact.

As always, Col. Wilcott was supportive, and I prepared the necessary paperwork for his signature. It seemed cruel to have to search a safe haven from the Army I'd once served so proudly and I knew my request was a shot in the dark, but I felt it was one I had to take for my well-being.

I'd sent off the paperwork and was waiting for a response when I received a phone call that caught me completely off guard. I'd just arrived at work one morning and was heading out of my office for a cup of coffee. Although I'm not really much of a coffee drinker, I enjoy morning conversations with Samantha and Marie. It gives me a chance to hear what's going in their lives, and they're always interested in what's happened in the previous night's officiating. As you can imagine, referees and umpires see a lot of human nature, and have some pretty good stories to tell!

Anyway, I was almost out the door when my phone rang and I turned back to answer it.

"Major Fischer. Can I help you?"

"This is Sergeant Carter from the IG office, ma'am."

The minute I heard the words "IG office," I could feel my body tense. What did they want?

"Ma'am, I'm calling to inform you that the Senior Review Panel will be here in Honolulu, and we want to know if you would be interested in meeting with a panel member."

I was stunned. Getting to talk to someone on the Senior Review Panel—the group commissioned by the Army after the Aberdeen scandals? This was great!

"Yes," I said, "I would certainly be interested in meeting with a panel member. But tell me if you can, Sergeant Carter, how did you get my name and number?"

"From Colonel Daigo, ma'am." Col. Daigo was an IG officer in Hawaii whom I'd met during my visits to the IG office here, and although he'd never interviewed me directly, he was familiar with my case.

After Sgt. Carter explained the process of setting up my appointment with a panel member, I thought of another question to ask.

"Do you know if the panel members will be meeting with personnel at the Army Medical Center? These are the people who deal with the counseling side of the house for women who are victims of sexual assault and harassment. It seems logical the panel would want to speak to them."

I heard the rustle of paper through the phone line. "No, ma'am, I don't see them on the schedule."

Although I was disappointed with that answer, I was certainly psyched about my own chance to sit down for a one-on-one discussion with a panel member. In the days that followed, I put together another informational notebook of what I saw as major issues and concerns for women in the military dealing with sexual harassment and assault. The notebook included a summary of my concerns, supporting articles from newspapers, and recommendations for policy changes.

It rained the day I headed out to Schofield Barracks for my appointment. There'd been an accident ahead of me, and the freeway was gridlocked. *Oh, no, I'm going to be late!* Fortunately, I'd carried my cell phone out of the office, so I called ahead to let someone know my predicament.

"No problem, ma'am, they're running a little behind schedule." *Whew!*

I did arrive late, but Command Sgt. Maj. Charleson, the panel member I would speak to, had just finished seeing her last appointment. I was ushered immediately into an office, and we sat down at a small conference table and got right into it.

I recounted my story and outlined my experiences of the past few years and then, for the next several hours, we discussed the issues that concerned me. She took notes while I emphasized the need for improved sexual harassment policies and for better counseling and separation options—for victims. And I expressed my surprise that the panel wouldn't be talking to personnel at the medical center.

I also reiterated my concerns about military leadership. "They say 'zero tolerance,' but that's not the way it works. The problem gets swept under the carpet and passed down from commander to commander."

Another topic I brought up was the need for victims to have legal counsel. And I questioned the unrealistic statutes of limitation soldiers faced if they wanted to initiate civil sexual harassment cases.

"Plus, I recommend a mentoring program," I said, "a quarterly program that would allow young women in the Army to talk to senior women about concerns and issues."

Before I left, I handed her the notebook, and she assured me that she would talk with the General Officer on the panel and would call me when she returned to Washington D.C. I never did get that call, which didn't surprise me.

In March, Army officers in Hawaii were in the process of completing what the military called Prevention of Sexual Harassment Training or POSH. The training packet originally came with a video that included Command Sergeant Major McKinney addressing soldiers on the topic of sexual harassment. Oops! The Army had to pull that one in a hurry, when Command Sgt. Maj. McKinney was charged with harassment himself in early February, shortly after the video went out.

POSH was what we call a chain teaching program— a slide show, with notes read by your commander, to all soldiers in your organization or unit. From my perspective, it was a white-wash job. I believe soldiers *know* what actions constitute sexual harassment. The problem is that when they (and *they* is usually but not always women) report harassment, no action is taken. The allegations either disappear completely, or they aren't taken seriously. And then the Army wonders why so few soldiers come forward! I kept hoping for a program that would make a real difference.

It wasn't long after POSH training that Col. Wilcott stopped by my office. A busy man, he almost never came by for idle conversation. So I knew something was up when he said, "If you have a minute, I'd like to talk to you."

I sensed his uneasiness as he lowered himself to the chair across from my desk. "Have you heard anything on your paperwork, Major?"

"No, sir. I'm afraid to call. I guess it has taken some time, but I suppose the paperwork will come in the mail soon."

He dropped his gaze briefly. "Well, we got the word today. I just got off the phone with Headquarters and it seems MP Branch has disapproved your request to stay with the Corps of Engineers."

My heart sank. *What now? Will I have to request a medical discharge?*

"This is not the end of it, Major Fischer," the commander assured me. "I'll talk to the Chief on his next visit and you can resubmit your request."

Against my will, tears began to well in my eyes. "Okay, sir. Thank you for letting me know, sir."

When he left my office, I let the tears flow. *When will this end? Why did MP Branch disapprove my request?* At that moment I felt like things would never get better, that the feelings of humiliation and betrayal would never go away. *I just can't go back to the MP world.* Once again, I felt imprisoned by the system. *He did the crime. I'm doing the time.*

"An Incident Like This"

After the MP Branch denied my request to stay with the Corps of Engineers, I looked more seriously into the possibility of a medical separation. During my year with Dr. Layton, I'd learned about a condition called Post-Traumatic Stress Disorder (PTSD). Although the public first became familiar with the term after the return of soldiers from Vietnam, PTSD sufferers also include people who survive natural disasters such as earthquakes or tornadoes; accidental disasters such as plane crashes; or manmade disasters such as child abuse, street violence, and sexual assault.

I have learned that many of the symptoms I've experienced since Panama—sleep loss and nightmares, irritability and outbursts of anger, short attention span—are common among people who've suffered trauma. Rape and sexual assault victims often experience particularly intense symptoms. In a study comparing rape victims with nonvictims, victims more often experience symptoms of fear, inability to feel and express emotions, disturbances of self-esteem, problems with parents and other authority figures, sexual dysfunction, and reduced effectiveness on the job for up to two years following the assault. (Kilpatrick, et. al., 1988; Koss & Burkhart, 1989) And when victims *know* their assaulters, they are more likely to blame themselves and rate themselves as less recovered than victims of rape by a stranger. (Katz & Burt, 1986)

Now I understand a great deal more about my reactions to Lt. Col. Smith's sexual assault. I wasn't crazy or neurotic; I was only exhibiting many of the symptoms of a "normal" assault victim. But I still didn't really *want* a medical separation. I knew that some women who had gone before medical review boards had been labeled with personality disorders when in reality they were suffering from PTSD. It seems clear, the abusers are the ones with the personality disorders! However, if the Army really was planning to send me back to the MP world, a medical separation might be my only option.

Dr. Layton had been talking to her contacts at the Army Medical Center about the medical separation process. This would involve seeing a military doctor for a diagnosis, then going before a medical review board, usually a randomly selected group of non-medical officers. I'll never forget the summer day when Dr. Layton told me that her contact in the Army Medical Center's psychiatric department didn't recommend that I use their system because it wasn't sensitive to my type of case. He (or perhaps she) recommended that I find another way to leave the Army.

"Who?" I snapped. "I want to know *who* said this about the Army medical system." *If people inside the system feel this way, they need to speak out!*

Dr. Layton paused for a moment. "I can't tell you, Linda. Our conversation was off the record."

"Off the record?" I could feel myself heating up. "If people can't stand behind what they say, they need to look for another line of work. When you become a part of that game, you are part of the problem. *Who* said it?"

"I'm sorry, Linda, I can't tell you."

I thought I was going to explode. "I just don't believe it! If no one will say anything, how are things supposed to get better? On the one hand, Medical Command is saying provisions for people like me are adequate, while people in the field are contradicting that opinion by recommending that I don't use the system."

That day I left Dr. Layton's office about as angry as I'd ever been. Although she felt honor bound not to reveal her sources, I could not agree. Nothing would ever change if we didn't all stand up and fight. Over the next few weeks, my dreams grew more intense, and my moods darker. To add to my discouragement, Col. Wilcott was getting ready to leave. He'd been so supportive, and at this point in my life, I needed all the support I could get.

Ironically, Col. Wilcott's Change of Command ceremony opened the door for what was to prove a most rewarding encounter for me. The Chief of Engineers,

General Turino, flew to Hawaii to preside over the ceremony. I'd met him on a previous visit, because one of my responsibilities includes escorting dignitaries to and from various functions. We had hit it off and discovered a mutual passion—fishing.

"Who taught you how to fish?" he'd asked at one point.

"My grandmother," I replied. "While my dad was in Vietnam."

"My grandmother taught me to fish, too!" And we were off with stories about fishing with our grandmothers.

On this trip, however, I wasn't telling fish stories. With my mind preoccupied by what might lie ahead, I kept quiet when I drove the general and his aide from place to place.

The Change of Command Ceremony went well, and while my new commander, Col. Nelson and his wife Brenda, hosted a reception, I drove the Chief and his aide-de-camp to the airport. We checked in the luggage, and then I escorted the two men to the Governor's Hospitality Room where they would wait until departure time. During our walk through the terminal, the Chief handed me a bronze coin. I stopped and looked at it curiously. One side featured a castle surrounded by the words 'United States Army Corps of Engineers.' I turned the coin over and saw three stars plus the unit insignia and the words 'Presented by Commanding General Chief of Engineers.'

As I clutched the coin in my hand, General Turino bent his tall frame toward me and said, "Linda, I want you to know you have my support. I want you to resubmit your paperwork and send it directly to my office for my endorsement. I know you have experienced many obstacles, but keep your head up. You're a good soldier. Again, you have my support."

"Thank you, sir," I managed to say over a huge lump in my throat. I put the coin away, but when I waved goodbye to the general and his aide, one hand was curled around that coin in my pocket. I sensed his words had been genuine, and I felt a surge of hope. His words echoed in my mind as I drove home. "Linda, I want you to know you have my support."

Anyone visiting my apartment would never know I'm in the military because I don't keep any reminders where I can see them. No pictures on the wall, no uniform jacket or hat, no awards. Everything is out of sight. Except for the Chief of Engineer's coin, which lies on my living room bookshelf—the only item from my time in the military that I choose to display.

In August of 1997, I resubmitted my request to stay and work with the Corps of Engineers. Following the Chief's instructions, I forwarded the paperwork directly to Headquarters for his endorsement. After I called to ensure his office had received my request, all I could do was wait with growing anxiety. Although I never doubted that the Chief's pledge of support was sincere, MP Branch could still disapprove the request.

September 9, 1997. Nothing could have prepared me for what I encountered that day. A thick envelope lay on my desk when I arrived at work. *At last! The IG report that I requested in February.*

I opened the package and leafed through the pile of documents. Here was my original letter to the IG, a transcript of the telephone interview, other papers. *Where is the response from the Medical Command? The one I specifically requested?* I rifled through the documents again before I called the IG office to protest.

"Send in a request for the memo," I was told.

I don't think so! "It took seven months to get this package and the one memo I specifically requested isn't included."

After pulling my request, the representative at the other end of the line admitted I had a point and promised to fax me the memo the following day, after clearing her action with the Legal Department. I hung up with a sigh of disgust and continued my perusal of the documents on my desk. *What was this? A journal of some kind with dates and lots of blacked out words and lines?*

I soon realized I was reading notes from the IG

representative's inquiry. The representative had obviously reviewed the CID report and then gone on to interview the officer who'd made the final decision in the disposition of the CID case. Although all names and some other words were blacked out, what I *could* read filled me with rage.

According to the IG representative, the adjudicating officer (I'll call him XXX) "came to the conclusion of putting a GOLOR (General Letter of Reprimand) in Smith's local file.... XXX was presented convincing written testimony (coupled with the CID ROI witness statements) that caused him to seriously doubt Fischer's credibility. However, (*and the next line is blacked out*)..., therefore, a GOLOR was written. When asked why he didn't take more of a drastic action, he stated that the process led him to believe that Fischer was partly to blame, that she was not as innocent *as the CID investigation portrayed her to be*, and therefore "*I didn't want to ruin Smith over an incident like this.*"

I could hardly believe what I was reading. What was the "convincing written testimony"? Did it come from Lt. Col. Smith? Why had I never been given an opportunity to rebut it? XXX had never contacted *me!* Why had he chosen to support Lt. Col Smith, even though the CID investigation substantiated the case? What about the doctor's letter? And how had he dared to conclude: "I didn't want to ruin Lt. Col. Smith *over an incident like this*" as if it were a purse snatching? The events that XXX so callously labeled "an incident" had certainly ruined *my* career and, if I hadn't taken action to heal myself, might have destroyed my life. With the anger that fueled me at that moment, I think I could have run a five minute mile straight up a mountain!

Given my shock over what I'd just read, the Medical Command response that I received the following day was something of an anti-climax, and I wasn't a bit surprised to read that "the MEDCOM does not believe an alternate mental health care system for soldiers in sensitive positions or those who may have fears of 'stigma' if they openly access existing mental health services is required."

So--here was the deal. MEDCOM didn't think

victims needed alternative mental health services, although someone at our local medical center didn't think the system was sensitive to women in my situation. And MP Branch had decided I would be going back to the environment that had left me needing mental health services in the first place. What an endless circle of dead ends!

Is Sorry Good Enough?

Knowing that my second request to remain with the Engineers might be denied, I paid another uncomfortable and humiliating visit to the head of psychiatry at the Army Medical Center. No matter how I felt about military counseling services, I would need the testimony of a military doctor if I were forced to pursue a medical separation. By October, I'd begun a counseling program at the Naval Station. Entering a military facility, sitting out in the hallway, filling out the required forms—all made me deeply anxious, but I knew I had to do this.

As I told my story to my new counselor, Dr. Sikes, I noticed an interesting change. Tears came to my eyes, but I didn't completely fall apart. Perhaps I was gaining some strength. Perhaps I was ready to work on some new issues—my extreme discomfort with attending Army functions, for example.

In 1996, I decided to attend the Engineers' Ball. I'd felt some uneasiness about going, but Jim agreed to come with me, which greatly reduced my tension. In 1997, I had hoped to go to the ball again with Jim, but unfortunately, he would be off-Island that evening. I knew I couldn't go alone, so I asked Samantha if she would join me. She agreed, and we decided to send in our reply cards and checks together.

My nightmares returned that very night, vivid as ever. I didn't sleep much for the next few nights, and I felt the return of old anxieties. Finally I had to request a short leave. *What's happening to me? I thought I'd gone beyond this. Why are my dreams still so violent and intense?* Working with Dr. Sikes, I learned that recurring PTSD symptoms are quite common and can be triggered by a variety of events. Just knowing that my reactions were normal, however, didn't alleviate their pain.

During my leave, Samantha called me for assistance in completing an action we were working on, and I volunteered to stop by the office later that day. When I arrived, she returned my check for the Engineers Ball.

"My husband and I won't be able to attend this year," she said. "I wanted to give your check back so you could send it in with your reply card."

"Thanks, Samantha." I breathed a sigh of relief and tore that check into a hundred pieces. That night, no dreams haunted me. But I never know exactly what events will blindside me with flashbacks or nightmares.

Surely, I thought, there's not much chance of having an unpleasant experience at a function hosted by the Girl Scouts. I might be unable to shake my aversion to military functions, but this was the Girl Scouts honoring women in the military, and I'd been invited to attend by Dr. Young, my supportive friend from DACOWITS. After all, I was once a Brownie and a Girl Scout.

Walking from my apartment to the Hilton Hawaiian Village where the event would be held, I began to have second thoughts, however. Here I was, with passersby eyeing my uniform, about to sell the Army to a group of young girls. Although the Army had provided me with some great opportunities, and my friends and associates considered me a success, could I honestly recommend a military career to girls? After the brutality of the last few years? When I wanted out, when I wanted to erase this part of my life and move on? Was this honorable? I hesitated at the corner of the elegant hotel.

A group of uniformed Girl Scouts lined the walkway before me, waving wildly. After I glanced back over my shoulder, I realized they were waving at *me*. "Welcome," they cheered. I couldn't turn back now, so I moved down the line, shaking hands and asking names. Some of the girls were shy, some were outspoken, but all had fresh faces, hope-filled eyes, and their whole lives ahead of them. I saw each one as an incentive to change things in the Army.

Inside the banquet room, I ran into Dr. Young. "Linda, glad to see you," she said warmly. "We're not quite ready to start so if you've got a minute, there's someone I want you to meet."

Out in the hallway, I waited while she disappeared
into a smaller room. Although I didn't know who Dr. Young
wanted me to meet, I suspected it might be a DACOWITS
representative. Soon she poked her head out the door and
invited me into the room, which turned out to be where the
VIPs were gathering before the banquet.

"Admiral Chambers, this is Major Fischer," Dr.
Young said and then immediately left me alone with a
medium-height red-haired woman in a white uniform. A
Navy admiral. I smiled politely, wondering what this officer
wanted with me.

Her first words deepened my confusion. "Major
Fischer, I told Dr. Young I wanted to speak to you when she
mentioned you would be here tonight. I just want to say I'm
sorry. I reviewed the case many times."

"Thank you for your concern, ma'am." I didn't want
to admit that I wasn't sure why the admiral wanted to talk to
me. DACOWITS had made it clear that they didn't take on
individual cases, so why had she reviewed my case?

"Are you doing okay?" she asked, looking at me
intently.

"I'm surviving, ma'am." *What's this all about?*

Ever so slowly the fog began to clear as she continued. "When Lieutenant Colonel Smith came into my office
to see me, we agreed he should retire, although we normally
just send these officers back to the appropriate branch of the
service and let them deal with the problem. Then after the
Aberdeen scandal broke, I felt I had made the wrong decision."

I was beginning to get the picture. I'd heard that
right before he retired, Lt. Col. Smith worked in a joint
personnel office that included all service branches, but
hadn't known who his superior was.

"He worked for you, ma'am?" Part of me didn't
want to hear her answer.

"Not directly, but he did work in the section I had
responsibility for at that time, so I spoke to him. His wife
was very ill, and considering the circumstances, we thought
it best he retire."

I was speechless, although plenty of words—some of them ugly ones—ran through my mind. A woman, a woman, had provided oversight on this case. My career had been curtailed—I'd certainly never be promoted again—and my personal life had been nearly destroyed. And he got to retire because his wife was ill? I'd known most of this before, of course, but not that his superior had been a woman. A woman who had known about my charges when she let him escape with full benefits. The news was devastating! I kept my head down and my clenched fists behind my back.

"Again, I want to say how sorry I am."

Although I didn't doubt the sincerity in her voice, I needed to get away. "I should go, ma'am."

When I turned to leave, I looked into her eyes and saw regret there. I'm sure she saw the pain in mine. It broke my heart to realize that a woman had, however inadvertently, perpetuated the cycle of abuse in the Army, and as I stumbled back into a room filled with laughing girls, I vowed to do my part to break that cycle.

Looking to the Future

The 1997 holiday season arrived, and Jim and I celebrated together again. Although I love Christmas in the Islands, the fear that this would be my last haunted me. The Army must have ruled on my IPCOT request by now, I thought, but why wasn't I hearing something? No news was generally bad news.

In early January I attended a Law Enforcement Conference in Washington D.C., where the weather was bitterly cold. I couldn't seem to get warm, and I wasn't sleeping well either. That first day at the conference, spent in a roomful of military police, was unbearably uncomfortable.

The officers in training with me seemed to ask so many questions. "Where were you on your last assignment? How long were you there? Who did you work for?" I kept thinking, *they're trying to put the pieces of the puzzle together. They know I'm the Fischer who charged Lt. Col. Smith, and they're hoping that if they ask enough questions, they'll get the answers.* Whenever possible I turned the conversational focus back on the questioner, and if someone did manage to pin me down, I answered as briefly as possible. But I couldn't stop drifting back to a place I longed to forget, and soon I found myself avoiding the company of others altogether, except to maintain a minimum of social politeness.

During the second day of the conference, a major I'd not met before approached me. "The assignments officer at MP Branch asked me to give this to you." He handed me a piece of paper. Glancing down, I recognized the cover sheet for my IPCOT request. I sucked in a deep breath and looked for the line that would tell me my fate. Good news at last! My request had been approved! For a moment or two I felt wildly happy.

Then doubts crept in. *Wait a minute...what does*

'approved' mean? Does it mean I can stay in Hawaii and in my current job with the Corps of Engineers or does it mean I can stay in Hawaii but I'll have to cross the street and work with the Military Police Corps?

I knew I couldn't celebrate until I'd cleared up that question. So I went to the lobby to call the assignment officer at MP Branch, even though, after our go-round when they disapproved the request the first time, picking up the phone wasn't exactly easy. I pulled a chair toward me, so I'd be sitting down, no matter what the news.

"This is Major Summers, can I help you?"

My throat felt dry. "Yes, this is Major Fischer, I just received the paperwork you sent over, and I have two questions about it."

"Go ahead."

"When it says the IPCOT is approved, does that mean I will stay with the Corps of Engineers in the same job?" A knot the size of a grapefruit sat in the pit of my stomach. And in the split second before he answered, I think I must have prayed a thousand times: *please God, let it be yes.*

My prayers were answered. "Yes, it does."

I leapt from my chair, feeling a smile split my face. "Okay, so that means my adjusted departure date will be three years from my current end date, taking me to the year 2001?"

"Yes, that is correct."

I hung up the phone and jumped around with excitement for a few minutes before bounding back into the conference room. I wouldn't have to subject myself to a medical review board after all, because I knew that as long as I was with the Corps of Engineers—my safe haven—I could survive. By 2001, I'd be within months of retirement.

During the lunch break, I dashed to the first pay phone I could find and called Jim. Unfortunately he was out on the road for the day, but I left a message in a voice that bubbled with excitement. "Call me when you can, I have good news!"

I knew I had the Chief of Engineers to thank for this

change in orders, so I stopped by his office, which was in
the same building as our training room. The Chief's aide,
who had expressed his support during his Hawaii trip, could
tell immediately that I'd received the good news, and when I
told him I planned to send a thank you card to the Chief, he
said, "I tell you what, we're running ahead of schedule
today. How about I get you in to see the Chief for a few
minutes so you can thank him yourself?"

Walking into that office and shaking the tall
officer's hand, I felt like I was in a dream come true. I
thanked him fervently for his support, and I know he could
see the happiness on my face.

After our first few words, he invited me to sit down
at his small conference table. "I am glad that I was able to
help with this," he said. "You've been through a lot in the
past few years."

I couldn't argue with that, but I did admit how
worried I'd been that MP Branch would refuse my request
again. "It wasn't that I doubted your support, sir. My doubts
were with the MP Corps. In spite of my pleas, they made it
very clear that the needs of the Army were driving the train,
so words simply can't express how grateful I am for your
support, sir."

"It was a pleasure to help," he responded, "and I
know you will do great things for the Engineer Corps."

Leaving his office, feeling some certainty in my
future, I experienced an indescribable sense of relief.
Although I knew I'd never have the career I'd once hoped
for, at least now I wouldn't have to face a medical board.
What a blessing! And the day's blessings hadn't ended yet,
for Chaplain Tim Bennett and I had planned to meet for
dinner. Back in my hotel room, I shed my uniform and
pulled on jeans and a sweatshirt, then picked up the TV
remote to channel surf until time to meet Tim. I must have
drifted off to sleep, because the ring of the phone startled me.

"Well, good evening, Linda," Jim's cheerful voice
brought me wide awake. "How is my princess? You sounded
pretty excited on the phone, so I thought I'd take a chance of
catching you on the phone before I go out on the night runs."

"You're not going to believe it," I bubbled. "I just got the word on my consecutive overseas tour and it was approved!"

Together we celebrated long distance, signing off with love and relief, and when Tim called from the lobby moments later, I was still jubilant. I managed to wait, however, until he and I were seated at a table in a small Thai restaurant before I shared my good news.

"Tim, I have to thank God for a small miracle. You are not going to believe this! Remember how, when we last talked, I told you that my consecutive overseas tour had been disapproved? Well, I reapplied and with the support of the Chief, it was approved."

Tim shared my excitement, and we spent a happy evening, reminiscing about San Antonio days and catching up on the news of old friends, especially Randy and Sarah McCarthy. While we talked, I ate with an appetite that would not quit. That night I slept soundly, too, for the first time in months.

So I returned to Hawaii, finding comfort in the certainty of my assignment and increasing hope for my future. I'll never forget what happened in Panama, of course, and I don't know when (or even if) the PTSD symptoms will disappear completely. But I am well on my way to personal recovery and am thankful for my job, my good friends, and the opportunity to live in this beautiful place. When I retire from the Army, I'd like to stay here in Hawaii and find a way to work with young people who are looking for a start in life. Sometimes we just need help getting our foot in the door, so that's what I'd like to do—help young people get their foot in the door.

Now that my life is moving forward, I find I can look back over my military career and appreciate the good parts. My deepest satisfaction is that I achieved so many of the goals I set. Early in my Panama tour a major I reported to asked me about my goals.

"I want to be selected to command a unit, finish my master's degree, and finish the Command and General Staff College (CGSC) through correspondence, before the majors' selection board in 1994."

I'll never forget his response. "Don't you think your goals are unrealistic? You should give those goals some thought."

I didn't know what to say. I'd set my goals high and was determined to reach them, but here my superior sounded like he was trying to discourage me. Well, not only did I accomplish my goals, I exceeded them! During that tour, I had two commands, finished my master's and CGSC, all before the board.

Although I don't regret joining the Army, I do wish the system were less supportive of the old order. When one man, chose to cross a line in a way that nearly destroyed my life. I found myself completely alone. Sometimes I wish that I had gone directly to the hospital or to some authority immediately. But I don't waste much time beating myself up about that, particularly when the newspapers tell us stories every day of female soldiers who *did* report assaults sooner than I did, but ended up getting the same results from the military system. Recently I read a quote from a woman soldier that speaks volumes: "You can report it, but they get you sooner or later."

Actually, I try not to spend my time regretting the past—what I did or didn't do. Instead I look at the positive. After all, Lt. Col. Smith did *not* destroy me. I *survived.* Now I see that survival, which I attribute to the fighter in me, as my greatest achievement. What happened was *wrong,* so I refused to throw in the towel, although I never dreamed the fight would go on so long.

Recognizing and acting on my deepest values— not giving up, fighting for what I believe to be right—has been instrumental in my recovery as a person. So has writing this book. Putting it all down—the good, the bad, the ugly—has allowed me to work through my experiences and to take a fresh look at my hopes for my future.

And what about my hopes for the Army, the institution I joined so eagerly sixteen years ago? To be honest, I think we have a long way to go. There are a few hopeful signs. Recently the Army initiated a program called

"Consideration of Others" to combat the problems of discrimination within the organization. "Consideration of Others " is a command program designed to increase every soldier's awareness of human relations issues and commitment to professionalism towards others. A "successful human relations climate" is defined as one that maximizes soldiers awareness of how their individual actions affect others, emphasizes respect between and for soldiers of all races, creeds, gender, or national/ethnic heritage, and enables soldiers to clearly understand the linkage between their actions toward others and their units' ability to accomplish the mission.

I support this training initiative as a productive means to learn the differences of all people and promote an environment in which everyone can work free of harassment and discrimination.

I believe it is time for Army leaders to take a serious look at current policies and procedures in the adjudication of cases, as well as the provisions for victims.

But will Army leadership make the hard decisions necessary to convince women that the military is a safe place? We need only look at the events of the spring of 1998 for the answer.

For weeks the eyes of the nation focused on the court martial of Sergeant Major Gene McKinney. Headlines screamed from daily newspapers, TV coverage was almost continual. A TV clip of a taped conversation between McKinney and one of the accusers held the spotlight for weeks. During the court martial, the media raised important questions as they had during the Aberdeen scandal. *Did* pervasive misuse of authority and abuse of power exist? *Were* allegations covered up on a regular basis? *Were* Army leaders betraying the trust of their troops?

Before the McKinney case closed, the highest ranking officer in the Aberdeen scandal was sentenced to just four months in prison under a plea agreement in which he pled guilty to adultery and sodomy and was cleared of the more serious charges of rape, indecent assault, and obstruction of justice. One of the enlisted men, Sergeant Simpson, was sentenced to 25 years in prison.

It was no surprise that lawyers for Command Sgt. Maj. McKinney began to argue that the military had a dual standard: one for enlisted personnel and one for officers. They might have had a point, but then the eight-member jury acquitted McKinney of 18 of 19 criminal charges. I listened to the news that day with dismay, believing that the verdict would discourage women from reporting sexual harassment, and from what I read in the papers over the next few days, thousands of soldiers and civilians—both men and women—agreed with me. "Web survey: Most judge sentence light" read a headline in the April 13 *Army Times*. "Army acquittal sends chilling message," said the *LA Times*. All over the country, editorials and articles questioned the Army's resolve to deal with sexual harassment.

These opinion pieces from the media echoed the findings of the Army's own Senior Review Panel which stated in its final report: "the Army lacks the institutional commitment" to treat men and women equally. "Passive leadership has allowed sexual harassment to persist," it concluded.

The panel also had harsh words for the complaint process, finding that it "re-victimizes victims, making them feel as if they are to blame for the misconduct and that they will be tagged as troublemakers for reporting it." I knew what that felt like, and my heart went out to Brenda Hoster and the other women who had come forward in the McKinney case. They reported that instead of victim aid, they endured isolation and lack of support. When one women sought mental health counseling, she was told that records of that counseling could be subpoenaed for use in the court martial. And in the end, the system ignored the voice of its females, choosing to believe the word of one man with more power than six women who had nothing to gain—and everything to lose—by speaking out.

Not long after the McKinney case acquittals, General Hale, a high-ranking IG officer, was allowed to retire with full honors and benefits after allegations of sexual misconduct were brought forward. Once again the

Army refused to bite the bullet and model a change of policy by dealing with the problem at the highest levels.

However, I continue to fight. Right now I am preparing a letter for members of Congress and other special interest groups. It will emphasize the need for improved policies and provisions for military women who are victims of serious sex crimes and severe cases of sexual harassment and will go out with several attachments: the letters from the Army's Medical Command and the local medical center, and the excerpt from the IG report that relegates my experience to "an incident like this."

Sexual harassment is about power. It's about the *ultimate power* that those in positions of authority exercise over those below them, the power that Lt. Col. Smith chose to abuse that night in Panama. As we look to the future, how our leaders deal with this abuse of power will determine whether or not we eliminate this enemy within the ranks.

An Open Letter

Although I would certainly never have chosen some of my experiences, I've learned a lot because of them. One of my goals is to pass on what I've learned. If you are a young woman about to enter the world of work—whether the military, the business world, or perhaps a helping profession—here is my open letter to you.

Consider what I find to be the pillars of well-being: your personal growth, your health and fitness, and your financial stability. These three pillars helped me rebuild my life, and I believe they keep me less vulnerable to power plays like the one that led to my assault.

In the area of personal growth, you have to find what works for you. Find out who you are. Each of us was taught values and has beliefs that affect our way of thinking. Understand them. For example, I was taught to be a fighter, to stand up for what was right. As long as I repressed that value and did not report Lt. Col. Smith, I had great difficulties functioning. After I stood up for what I knew was right, my life didn't get a whole lot easier, but at least I could begin the recovery process for myself.

Discover what motivates you in life. Perhaps it's religious connections or conferences and seminars in your area of expertise or entrepreneur programs and literature. The latter works for me. *The Anthony Robbins' Personal Power 30 Day Program* was the jump start I needed, a dynamic program that helped me in all areas of my life.

But I emphasize again: look for what works for you. What makes you feel and do your best? The opportunities are limitless, so if you search, you will find. And you will discover that when you know who you are, what you like and dislike, you can do so much more in life. Take the energy that drives you and stay in touch with it.

Being continually aware of your state of mind is also important to your personal well-being. Where you are emotionally and how you are thinking affects how you interpret and respond to what is going on around you and those communicating with you. Have a group of friends you meet with regularly. This is so important because when life and circumstances get us down, our inclination may be to withdraw and isolate ourselves. The right friends will pick up on changes in our interactions and may be able to help.

I've often thought how unfortunate it was that Millie and other good friends left Panama shortly before the assault. I'd spent a lot of time with this group—going to lunch, movies, sporting events, talking on the phone—and I believe they would have noticed my withdrawal and personality change and reached out to me. The right friends will offer you the opportunity to pour out your troubles, which might be just what you need in difficult times. I used to think it was so amazing the way my friend Debbie drops by whenever I am having a real bad hair day. Recently I learned her visits aren't just coincidences. The secretaries notice my moods and call her when they think I could use some support. Being around a strong peer group—people whose judgment you respect and trust and who care about you—can help you shore up your own self-esteem during times when outside forces are battering at it.

I also suggest mentoring programs as an avenue for discussing hard issues and concerns in your line of work. It's another forum to head off concerns before they become problems. Choose role models and learn from them. They are a great source of information and usually very willing to share ideas and thoughts. Most people are just afraid to ask.

Another component of personal growth is your ability to talk to others and communicate your thoughts. I personally like the book *Tongue Fu* by Sam Horn. It's a great book, designed to help you keep your foot out of your mouth! She describes situations which could be very difficult and then gives you suggestions on how to get out without digging a deeper hole for yourself. Many of her tips have helped me when I've had to react to uncomfortable situations involving my case. And I've also found them useful for dealing with coaches while I'm officiating games. Now I'm able to defuse the situation, rather than escalate the problem. *How to Win Friends & Influence People* by Dale Carnegie is another one of my favorites for developing communication skills.

When it comes to listening skills, Jim gave me what I think is the best rule to follow—bar none: never leave a signature. What does leaving a signature mean? Well, when someone expresses an opinion, most of us feel obligated to give our own. When you counter, you leave your signature. Just because you know how a person feels doesn't mean it's necessary to give them that information about yourself. If the person asks for your opinion, you might say, "You have an interesting point," or "Let me give that some thought." But the idea is to keep the focus on the other person and learn about them. If you must counter, be sure to choose the best time and technique to help them consider alternatives or look at the issue from another perspective.

You gain a lot of knowledge when you listen carefully to others. Like they always say—you can not talk and listen at the same time. So be a good listener. And then respond appropriately. If someone tells you that you look good, don't say, "I need to lose ten pounds": just say, "thank you."

Another good rule: do not be negative. If you can't say something good about the situation or person, don't say it. Yes, I know your mother always told you this, but occasionally she was right!

Finding what works for you also applies to the second pillar—health and fitness. When you exercise, where you exercise, when you eat, what you eat, how much you sleep—and so on. You have to find what works for you.

I know that I always feel my very best when I exercise regularly and watch what I eat. But this is no small task because I dearly love desserts. In fact, I'll run four miles three times a week, just so I can eat desserts. And that's only half the battle. I have to work at eating the well-balanced diet I know I need. To do this, I've set my own rules of the road that I try to follow. One of them is to drink a lot of water, and I now have bottled water delivered to the office, with a refrigerated dispenser. Another is to never eat after 7:00 in the evening. If the clock reads 7:01, I won't eat. But remember, this is just a rule that works for me. You will make your own rules.

I do believe, however, that there is one overarching principle that applies to all of us: when we are healthy and physically fit, we are better equipped to handle stressful situations. As my situation grew worse in Panama, I stopped exercising regularly, leaving no outlet for the frustration and stress building up inside of me. Because of my

negative association of sports with Lt. Col. Smith,
I eliminated many of the activities I had loved just at
the time when they might have done me the most
good. Now, as I continue to recover and rebuild my
life, I realize that the more I exercise and stay healthy,
the easier it is for me to handle uncomfortable situations.

Your financial stability is the third pillar and a
key factor in your overall well-being. Worrying about
how you are going to pay the next bill or about losing
your job will affect your decision-making process. In
Panama, my financial situation was good in that I had
a paycheck coming each month, but I felt my career
was at risk, that my boss held it in the palm of his
hand. I've often wondered if it was mere coincidence
that the assault occurred just months before the
promotion board, when one less than perfect report
would end my career.

If you are financially unstable, you're a soft
target. It's like applying for a loan. The bank will
check your debt to income ratio, and if that ratio is too
high, you don't qualify for the loan. You are considered vulnerable, at risk.

So be smart financially and minimize your
vulnerability. Watch your debt to income ratio.
I like the cash and carry rule. If I can't pay cash,
I can't have it. I particularly like those wonderful debit
cards. Using one is convenient and easy, but unlike
credit cards that build debt, a debit card is just like
writing a check. Have a good slush fund or savings
account for emergencies. And don't be afraid to start
small. You'll be surprised how fast a few dollars a
week will add up. Invest, invest, invest by paying
yourself first and then pay your bills. The sooner
you get started, the better—so start right away.

I'm quite a fan of financial planning books, and there are a number of good ones out there. For Christmas Jim gave me *Don't Worry, Make Money* by Richard Carlson, and it's absolutely my favorite book. In fact, I liked it so much that I turned around and bought one for him. Others I can recommend are *The Wealthy Barber* by David Chilton and *Wealth Without Risk* by Charles Givens.

My final suggestion for financial well-being: have more than one source of income, even if that income comes from something you do just a couple of hours a week. I know that I couldn't support myself (at least not in the style to which I am presently accustomed) on my shoe polish, officiating, and book mark enterprises, but because of these sidelines, I have the confidence that I will be able to support myself when I leave the Army. And confidence reduces vulnerability.

When you evaluate your pillars of well-being—personal, physical, and financial stability—look for balance. You may need to focus first on building up the weakest area, before that weakness brings the whole structure tumbling down. But then pay equal attention to all.

A final piece of advice: avoid situations in which you feel you do not have a choice. You can do this by learning to communicate assertively in unpleasant situations, by staying alert to the realities around you. And don't be complacent, believing that a serious crisis will never happen to you. Be vigilant and prepared. Use a mentor when you can, but understand that in the final analysis, it's up to you.

Before you step out into the workplace, be willing to ask yourself searching questions. Do you know yourself? Do you know what drives you? Are you stable financially—or at least not overwhelmed with debt? How well do you handle stress? How would you handle an uncomfortable work situation? Do you have friends you trust? Would they notice a change in your behavior? Who would you call if you needed help? And don't fool yourself into thinking you will never need help. Don't tell yourself, oh, I can play this game. Dealing with sexual harassment or any other serious crisis is not a game! So hone your skills, keep your eyes open, and go out there and show the world what you can do.

I wish you the very best.

Lynda

Suggested Reading List

Think & Grow Rich	Napoleon Hill
How to Win Friends and Influence People	Dale Carnegie
Don't Worry Make Money	Richard Carlson, Ph.D.
Tongue Fu!	Sam Horn
The Instant Millionaire	Mark Fisher
Even Eagles Need A Push	David McNally
The Wealthy Barber	David Chilton
Wealth Without Risk	Charles J. Givens
The 7 Habits of Highly Effective People	Stephen R. Covey
Chicken Soup for the Soul	Jack Canfield and Mark Victor Hansen
The Power of Positive Thinking	Norman Vincent Peale
Swim With The Sharks Without Being Eaten Alive	Harvey Mackay
Man's Search For Meaning	Viktor E. Frankl
Success Through A Positive Mental Attitude	W. Clement Stone
Believe and Achieve	Samuel A. Cypert
Victory Over The Darkness	Neil T. Anderson
Where is God When It Hurts? Disappointment With God	Philip Yancey
The Healthy Personality and The Christian Life	Douglas Hooker
Healthy Personality	Sidney Jourard and Ted Landsman
Create Work You Love	Nancy Hanson
Public Speaking Made Easy	Pam Chambers
Step Forward • Sexual Harassment In The Workplace	Susan L. Webb

Suggested Program

Personal Power! 30 Day Program	Anthony Robbins

Emotionally wrenching! Provoking! And, if a woman who has worn a uniform reads this dramatic story, perhaps she might say, "I have been there, too."

Having read "Ultimate Power Enenmy Within The Ranks" it is my prayer that having written her story, it will serve as a catharsis and allow Linda to go forward, not with a lack of faith in the Military Police Corps and the Army I love so dearly, but with hope and trust in the goodness of officers dedicated to DUTY, HONOR, COUNTRY.

While we live in an imperfect world, we must continuously strive to improve its shortcomings. Certainly, the military system must ensure that those to whom the lives of so many men and women have been entrusted, does not fall short because of the actions of a few. In God we trust! But in man, every woman in uniform must be assured of protection.

Although my name is not mentioned in "Ultimate Power Enemy Within The Ranks," I did advise Linda of the consequences of presenting her complaint following a lapsed period of time. However, my advice then and now is always have the courage to do what you feel is right and just, and may God be with you!

Sherian G. Cadoria,
Brigadier General, US Army, Retired

Please send _____ copies of
Ultimate Power: Enemy Within the Ranks to:

Name _____

Address _____

_____

City _____ State _____ Zip _____ - _____

Telephone _____ Fax _____

email _____

Book: $19.95 US$ $ _____
S&H: $4.00 and $2.00 for each add'l copy   _____
                                         Total: _____

Payment:
☐   Check or money order
☐   Credit card
   ☐ Visa   ☐ Mastercard   ☐ American Express

   Card number _____

   Name on card _____ Exp. date _____ / ____

   Signature _____

Fax/telephone orders: **808.921.9005**

Online orders: **orders@unlimited-inc.com**

US Mail orders: **Unlimited Inc.**
                        P.O. Box 89546
                        Honolulu, HI 96830-9546

Linda A. Fischer is available for keynotes and seminars.
Please call for additional information and schedule:
                    808.921.9005

                    visit our website
              www.unlimited-inc.com

Please send _____ copies of
Ultimate Power: Enemy Within the Ranks to:

Name _____

Address _____

_____

City _____ State _____ Zip _____ - _____

Telephone _____ Fax _____

email _____

Book: $19.95 US$ $ _____

S&H: $4.00 and $2.00 for each add'l copy   _____

                                 Total: _____

Payment:

☐ Check or money order

☐ Credit card

    ☐ Visa   ☐ Mastercard   ☐ American Express

    Card number _____

    Name on card _____ Exp. date _____ / ___

    Signature _____

Fax/telephone orders: **808.921.9005**

Online orders: **orders@unlimited-inc.com**

US Mail orders: **Unlimited Inc.**
P.O. Box 89546
Honolulu, HI 96830-9546

Linda A. Fischer is available for keynotes and seminars.
Please call for additional information and schedule:
808.921.9005

visit our website
www.unlimited-inc.com

Order Form

Please send _____ copies of
Ultimate Power: Enemy Within the Ranks to:

Name _____

Address _____

_____

City _____ State _____ Zip _____ - _____

Telephone _____ Fax _____

email _____

Book: $19.95 US$ $ _____
S&H: $4.00 and $2.00 for each add'l copy   _____
                                    Total: _____

Payment:
☐ Check or money order
☐ Credit card
    ☐ Visa   ☐ Mastercard   ☐ American Express

    Card number _____

    Name on card _____ Exp. date _____ / ____

    Signature _____

Fax/telephone orders: **808.921.9005**

Online orders: **orders@unlimited-inc.com**

US Mail orders: **Unlimited Inc.**
                        P.O. Box 89546
                        Honolulu, HI 96830-9546

Linda A. Fischer is available for keynotes and seminars.
Please call for additional information and schedule:
                        808.921.9005

visit our website
www.unlimited-inc.com

Bookmark

An uplifting and inspirational poem
about the importance of prayer

"If Jesus Had a Telephone"

If Jesus had a telephone
Would He accept my call?
or would He say "I'm busy,
Can't talk to you at all."
Would He use the same excuses
That we so often do
When we don't care to listen
To one who's feeling blue?
If I dialed Jesus' number
Would an angel answer there
And tell me "Jesus isn't in,
He's gone, I don't know where.
Could be He's hunting or fishing
Or watching a game of ball.
But if you'll leave your number
He will return your call."
If I could talk to Jesus
I know just what I'd say.
Forgive me, Lord and thank you
For guiding me each day.
Teach me to live for others
And give to those in need.
Help me show love and kindness
With every word and deed.
Till Jesus gets a telephone
I'll talk to Him in prayer.
I know He always listens
I know He's always there.
Our help and our salvation
Are in His hands alone,
So don't forget to say your prayers
Until Jesus gets a phone.

by Ella Stephens
© 1996 Fischer

Beautifully printed on blue marble paper

A Thoughtful Gift for Everyone

Excellent for Bible Studies & Prayer Groups

Unlimited Inc.
P.O. Box 89546
Honolulu, HI 96830-9546

Proshine

Professional Durable Shoe Polish

Instant Glossy Shine
available in
Black and Brown

Made in the USA

4 oz Bottle w/applicator
$5.50

To place an order

Call 808.921.9005

♣

use the handy Product Order Form
or
visit our website
www.unlimited-inc.com

Unlimited Inc.
P.O. Box 89546
Honolulu, HI 96830-9546

Product Order Form

Item	Qty	Cost/ea	Totals
Bookmark	_____	x $ 2.00	$ _____
5x7 poster	_____	x $2.50	$ _____
8x10 poster	_____	x $3.00	$ _____
Set (one ea)	_____	x $6.50	$ _____
Shoe Polish	_____	x $5.50	$ _____
Book	_____	x $19.95	$ _____
S/H @ $4. ($2/ea add'l copy)			$ _____
			$ _____

Name _____

Address _____

_____

City _____ State _____ Zip _____ - _____

Telephone _____ Fax _____

email _____

Payment:
- ☐ Check or money order
- ☐ Credit card
  - ☐ Visa ☐ Mastercard ☐ American Express

Card number _____

Name on card _____ Exp. date ____ / ____

Signature _____

Fax/telephone orders: **808.921.9005**

Online orders: **orders@unlimited-inc.com**

US Mail orders: **Unlimited Inc.**
P.O. Box 89546
Honolulu, HI 96830-9546

visit our website
www.unlimited-inc.com

Product Order Form

Item	Qty	Cost/ea		Totals
Bookmark	_____	x $ 2.00		$ _____
5x7 poster	_____	x $2.50		$ _____
8x10 poster	_____	x $3.00		$ _____
Set (one ea)	_____	x $6.50		$ _____
Shoe Polish	_____	x $5.50		$ _____
Book	_____	x $19.95		$ _____
S/H @ $4. ($2/ea add'l copy)				$ _____
				$ _____

Name _____

Address _____

_____

City _____ State _____ Zip _____ - _____

Telephone _____ Fax _____

email _____

Payment:
☐ Check or money order
☐ Credit card
   ☐ Visa   ☐ Mastercard   ☐ American Express

   Card number _____

   Name on card _____ Exp. date ____ / ___

   Signature _____

Fax/telephone orders: **808.921.9005**

Online orders: **orders@unlimited-inc.com**

US Mail orders: **Unlimited Inc.**
P.O. Box 89546
Honolulu, HI 96830-9546

visit our website
www.unlimited-inc.com